MORE THAN
A TROPHY

Dennis Walrod

Stackpole Books

MORE THAN A TROPHY

Copyright © 1983 by Dennis Walrod

Published by
STACKPOLE BOOKS
Cameron and Kelker Streets
P.O. Box 1831
Harrisburg, PA 17105

Printed in the U.S.A.

Library of Congress Cataloging in Publication Data
Walrod, Dennis.
  More than a trophy.

  Includes index.
  1. Game and game-birds, Dressing of. 2. Cookery (Venison) 3. Taxidermy.
4. White-tailed deer.
I. Title.
SK283.8.W34   1983   799.2'77357   83-8157
ISBN 0-8117-2255-4 (pbk.)

This book is dedicated to my wife, Peg, for her encouragement and enlightened criticism and for being able to translate my scribbling into a typed manuscript.

Contents

Chapter 1

After the Hunt ... What Else?

Beyond the Kill

The deer has fallen. That is the point at which this book begins. After the killing shot is fired, the echoes of that brief, violent moment quickly drift away, carrying with them the fatigue from the long hours of careful stalking and patient waiting. Silence fills the air, pushing away even the lingering aroma of burnt gunpowder. The hunt is over. The whitetail buck lies crumpled upon the earth, its mute form a testimony to the finality of the ultimate act of hunting. We are both elated and sad.

There is a philosophic conflict in our mixed emotions. Abiding by the standards of the sporting ethic, we agree that the act of killing a game animal is only one of the many reasons for engaging in the sport of hunting in this modern age. Yet, for how long would we continue to hunt if that one reason, the kill, were to be repeatedly denied us through poor luck and circumstance? One year? Ten years? A lifetime? The answer is personal, of course. We should each ask ourselves just how important the kill really is, for in our answer will be a measure of our commitment to the sport aspect of hunting. If we must always succeed in killing something, then we have failed in our sport.

Unlike small game hunting, in which an empty bag is of no more economic consequence than the cost of a pound or two of meat, deer hunting provides the possibility of a grand prize for success. Frankly, a whitetail deer is worth a lot of money. The value of two deer is roughly equivalent to the cost of a good deer rifle or shotgun and a pocketful of ammunition. Add a third deer and you can then cover the cost of boots, hunting clothes, a knife, and maybe even a tankful of gas. But, if we continue to think in these mercenary terms, as though deer hunting were a business enterprise, we would quickly lose our enjoyment of hunting. If we instead consider the value of a fallen deer from the point of view of a wise consumer, we can actually increase our overall appreciation of hunting. Particularly, if we do our own butchering, preserving, tanning, and handicrafts, using with the skills of our own hands the carcass of a fallen deer, we can justify our desire to succeed in dropping a deer because we will have extended the sport beyond the kill itself. And, in the future, our enjoyment of the sport will not culminate and then fade at the moment of the kill. If we are able to realize that within us is a responsibility to use a deer to the fullest advantage and value, we will have enhanced not only the worth of a deer, but our own worth as well.

The Whitetail Deer—A Renewable Resource

The whitetail deer is definitely not on the endangered species list. Far from it, in fact. The whitetail is so ecologically adaptable that the real problem is keeping deer populations down within controllable limits. We think of deer as creatures of the forest, and they are, but it is more accurate to think of deer as dwellers on the *edges* of the forest. Large tracts of mature woodlands offer very sparse food supplies to deer, whereas the bushy, brushy low growth of edge-type cover provides a cornucopia of foods that deer can easily obtain. Ironically, it was the white man's axe and the spread of civilization across America that improved, rather than destroyed, the whitetail habitat. As the land was settled and the forests were cleared to provide acreage for crops and farms, more edge cover was created and the deer population began to grow.

The whitetail deer became a major source of protein for the new

Fig. 1. The whitetail deer is a renewable natural resource if wisely managed and utilized. There are about 12 million deer in America. (Photo by Irene Vandermolen, courtesy of Leonard Lee Rue.)

and growing cities, serving as a temporary substitute for domesticated farm animals while American agriculture of the 19th century evolved from subsistence farming into more efficient and productive operations capable of feeding a growing nation. However, this uncontrolled market hunting eventually offset the original increase in the deer population that had begun over a century earlier. Finally, between 1890 and 1920, most states enacted laws to protect the whitetail deer, and it was during this same time that scientific principles of game management were first applied. Today, the various state game and conservation agencies can predict within a few percentage points what the annual harvest will be, and they have the necessary tools to help make these predictions come true, such as doe permit systems, the setting of seasons, and game law enforcement. Scientific management of deer herd size is directed towards achieving stable, rather than just "large," populations of whitetails. As a rule of thumb, the optimum deer population that can be maintained per square mile of deer habitat is about twenty deer. Too many deer can deplete the supply of browse faster than it can recover through natural growth. A smaller, well-fed deer herd can easily survive a harsh winter, but an overcrowded and undernourished deer herd faces the gruesome prospect of wholesale death from disease and starvation.

Hunting is the only means we have for preventing catastrophic swings in the deer population from too high to too low. Without hunting, the whitetail deer species conceivably could become endangered. In the absence of natural predators (chiefly the cougar and the wolf) and without the culling of the herd as was done by the Indians, there is no other feasible means of controlling deer populations other than by hunting.

Let's take a look at some very interesting numbers. The estimate of the total number of deer in America is now somewhere around twelve million. Remember this fact the next time that you're out in the woods during the deer season, wondering where all the deer have gone. A tally of the annual kill-by-state reveals that nearly two and a half million of these deer are killed each year by hunters. That's close to 20 percent of the total, or about one out of every five deer, that are harvested annually. These statistics are meaningless, of course, when you first see that buck (*your* buck!) come trotting into the clearing, sunlight glinting off his antlers as you raise the gun to aim and fire. But consider this: your deer contributes to a national larder of venison that annually totals nearly three-quarters of a *billion* dollars in value. That's based on average yields per deer, at prevailing prices for equivalent cuts of beef. The hides alone potentially contribute an extra twenty million dollars to that total. Obviously, deer hunting is a worthy enterprise, both because of its positive effect on the overall stability of the deer population and because of the contribution that it makes to our own personal kitchen-table economies. The whitetail deer is a renewable resource in the finest sense; it provides us with a challenging sport, serves as a valuable trophy, and yet successfully thrives undiminished along the fringes of civilization.

How Indians Used the Whole Deer

The complete utilization of the whitetail deer that was made by the eastern American Indian has set a standard that would be both difficult and impractical for modern man to attain. Nevertheless, the standard is there, representing a goal that we at least can respect and admire. Maybe, by looking into the dim and distant past, we can even pick up some ideas for the more complete utilization of our own modern deer.

Fig. 2. These well-racked whitetail buck make an attractive quartet. (Photo by Irene Vandermolen, courtesy of Leonard Lee Rue.)

The whitetail deer was a major source of meat for the Indians, and deer hunting parties were often huge and elaborate affairs involving hundreds of the members of a tribe. Sometimes long barriers and corrallike structures were built so that deer could be herded into them for slaughtering. Deer were also stalked one-on-one by lone hunters armed with bow and arrow, a technique that modern man (armed with a full stomach) considers to be more sporting. The Indians ate some of their venison as fresh meat, and although their vocabulary may have lacked words like "filet mignon," you can bet that they had an appreciation for the better cuts from a deer. (Can you imagine having to butcher a deer with no more than a sharp rock or bone for cutting?)

However, because of the unpredictability of the supply of fresh venison from week to week, a generous share of deer meat was made into pemmican, which is not unlike jerky. Thin strips of venison were dried in the sun and then pounded and shredded for mixing into a paste with melted venison fat. Berries were crushed into the pemmican, which added both flavor and the preservative qualities of sugar and fruit acids. When the bitter winds of winter blew long and hard, and the braves sat around the fire grumbling that it was too cold to go hunting, a good supply of pemmican was as good a reason as any to stay home and keep warm.

We all know that many items of clothing, blankets, robes, and moccasins were made from the hide of a deer. The tanning process consisted of first soaking the hide with a solution made from the brains of the deer, which left the skin smooth and supple after drying. Ropes could be braided from strips of hide, and certain of the tendons and intestines were also used as bowstrings, for attaching points to arrows and, no doubt, a variety of other uses, including sewing. There is considerable archaeological evidence that deer antlers were sometimes used as garden rakes by those tribes that practiced agriculture. Antler tines were also used as flint flakers in the manufacture of arrowheads. Several types of tools, including awls, needles, knives, combs, and fishhooks were made from the bones of the whitetail deer after the bones had been boiled for soup. Hooves were hollowed out for use as bell-like musical jangles and for cup and pin games by the fireside. Even the lower jaw of the deer found use as a scraping tool. The ribs were sometimes used in a wicker arrangement to add rigidity to mats and baskets.

Obviously, there wasn't much left of a deer when the Indians had used it to fullest advantage. Such complete utilization is no longer feasible as, indeed, it was no longer among the Indians after they were able to get the white man's cloth and steel tools. Now we all have television and Monday night football. Somehow, though, it seems that something very precious has been lost.

Reasons Why You Should Do-It-Yourself

The do-it-yourself concept is so ingrained into the hunting tradition that its basic tenets rate right up there with motherhood and apple pie. We find game unassisted by native beaters, perform minor gun repairs, reload ammunition, sometimes even load up our own sandwiches, and perform many other such tasks, all while studiously avoiding household chores. ("Call the plumber, dear. I'm going hunting".)

We often lose sight of the fact that the act of hunting is, in its own right, an expression of the do-it-yourself concept. Our willingness—nay, eagerness—to go into the wilderness in pursuit of wild game is no less than a symbolic gesture to the plastic world of modern supermarkets, and to the nice folks at the abattoir, that we-will-do-it-ourselves, thanks just the same. Prime time television can never compete with the real life adventures of a deer hunter. We are never more alive than when we are hunting. In the woodlands, we can see ourselves objectively as participants in a primordial drama that is much less complicated than filing an income tax return. We see ourselves belonging (however temporarily) to two worlds; one of the hunter and the other of mortgages and faulty plumbing. Too often, when the deer season comes to a close, the gun gets put back in the rack, our boots get shoved into a corner, and we go back to being mundanely domesticated. Our do-it-yourself motivations are channeled off into doing those other rather uninteresting chores that were deserted when the hunting season opened. But it doesn't have to be that way. With a little finesse (and maybe some fast talking, if necessary), we can milk the hunter's do-it-yourself formula for at least a couple of months or more of postseason projects.

Of course, there are other, far more practical reasons for doing all the work, such as processing a deer, by yourself, not the least of which is the fact that the job will get done, and be done correctly. Another reason can be found in simple economics. For example, the cost to have a deer carcass professionally butchered presently ranges between twenty to thirty dollars, plus you also forfeit ownership of the deer hide. The hide can be sold at many taxidermists' shops for between five to ten dollars, and that is money that might as well be going into your pocket rather than someone else's. Better yet, tan the hide yourself and it becomes even more intrinsically valuable for trophy or leathercraft use.

It is in the butchering itself that the most good (or harm) can be done to the quality of the venison. Ironically, this is one job that amateurs can often do better than professionals because venison does not lend itself to professional meat-cutting methods. Venison should be freed of all fat and bone in order to preserve good meat flavor. Most professionals, however, butcher deer in much the same way that they also process beef, pork, and lamb; that is, the entire carcass is sawed into separate sections, bones and all. Very often, the professionals do not bother to properly trim and discard the tallow (fat) from a deer carcass. Venison tallow (and bone marrow, which contains tallow) imparts a waxy off-taste to venison during cooking. Tallow also shortens freezer life and eventually spoils the natural good flavor of the lean meat. This may very well be the major reason that many people claim to not like venison; they tried it once, didn't like the tallow taste, and saw no reason to ever try venison again. There are, of course, folks who have been eating tallow with venison all their lives and who still like venison regardless of the waxy taste. I offer no argument against personal preferences. However, the fact remains that the savory appeal of venison lean meat is apt to be better appreciated by a wider range of people if the tallow and bone are removed during butchering. This is really a simple procedure, although it is somewhat time consuming. Professional meat cutters can't afford that extra time and effort, at least not without charging you a higher rate. Even at present operating costs, most professional butchers must rely on a high speed bandsaw to do nearly all their cutting. The effect of such a saw on a deer carcass is that the cut surfaces become smeared with tallow and bone chips. The venison will still be edible and perhaps almost good tasting, but it won't be delectable, and that certainly makes a difference at mealtime. The boneless butchering technique described in chapter 6 permits the quick dismantling of a deer carcass into smaller, more easily handled sections without the use of a saw, except in one strategic location where the meat is unaffected by sawing. Sound easy? It really is.

By doing the butchering yourself, other benefits are also gained. For one thing, there can be no question as to whether the meat all comes from your deer only. This is not to say that a professional butcher will cheat you; that is possible, but highly improbable. However, identification tags can be misplaced, packages can accidentally be mislabeled, and who is to know for certain that one pile of venison burger belongs to you and not to someone else? At any rate, you take home what they give you.

Doing your own wrapping for the freezer also has definite advantages. Besides being fun, you gain control over what the sizes of the various serving portions will be. Wrapping is the nicest stage of the butchering process; this is when the rewards of your efforts are most apparent — when the steaks and roasts are piled high. You can carefully and lovingly divvy up these treasures into smaller piles that each represent a meal. You match up steaks by size and type, meanwhile planning for picnics, backyard grilling, candlelight suppers, and so on; it is difficult not to think of eating when you are playing with food. Most venison roasts need to be rolled and tied, and this job is best done by two people — one to hold and fold the meat into a spherical or oblong roast, while the other person wraps and ties the meat into place with string. Be sure to label each package as it is wrapped so that there won't be any surprises later in the year. I know of one fellow who received his professionally butchered and wrapped deer in packages that were so illegibly marked that every venison meal was a surprise. By doing your own wrapping and labeling, you can also organize several future meals. There might be a certain cut of venison that strikes your fancy for marinating, a fondue, or perhaps for a special occasion. Mark the appropriate comments on the wrapper and later (if you can still read your own handwriting) proceed with those original good ideas.

Of course, not all the bounty from the butchering and processing of a deer goes into the freezer. There is also the intangible reward of learning from the firsthand experience of doing your own butchering that meat doesn't grow in plastic trays. In the homes of many deer hunters, butchering is a family affair in which spouse and children share in the chores of stocking the larder. A sense of mutual accomplishment is a natural side benefit of these efforts. After all, only a few decades or so have passed since the era when home butchering was last a part of everyday American life. People in those earlier days weren't confused about where their meat came from ("Go fetch a chicken, Wilma."), and they probably saw nothing particularly remarkable about the home-learned butchering skills that they applied. Butchering was just another chore, not a big deal. Modern meat processing and marketing methods have done wonders for our food distribution systems, but they also have wrecked our sense of personal involvement and perhaps have even lessened our full appreciation of quality meat. By doing your own venison butchering, you gain a better understanding of what quality is — in this case, a better hunt, a better steak, and a fuller appreciation of the whitetail deer as a worthy game animal.

Similarly, amateur taxidermy, hide tanning, leathercraft, and other handicrafts are rewarding pastimes which enhance the appreciation of hunting. Trophies come in many forms. Antlers can be scored, but there is no equivalent Boone and Crockett scoring system for measuring a pride of accomplishment. Utilize a deer to your fullest advantage and, by doing that, learn the full meaning of the word "trophy."

Chapter 2

Tools and Equipment for the Deer User

Keeping It Simple

It's easy to go too far with this matter of tools and equipment. There are so many ingenious gadgets on the market that a deer hunter could buy several new items every year and still be left with the vague feeling that his hunting, butchering, and other related endeavors were somewhat less than class acts.

Of course, equipment needs are really determined by how far from home you are hunting and by the extent to which you will be processing a deer (assuming you get one) once you are back in camp or at home. In all situations, however, simplicity is usually the best route to follow. Make sure that you have the basic utensils first, and then, when you have learned to properly use them, you can more wisely begin collecting all those other contraptions and devices that we so dearly love to possess.

The majority of whitetail deer are felled within a mile of a roadway, so it doesn't make good sense to carry into the woods all the paraphernalia that probably won't get used there anyway. Leave the hatchet, the portable block-and-tackle, the cheese cloth, folding meat saw, and all that other stuff in the vehicle or in camp. Unless you have backpacked into a remote wilderness region and truly need certain tools for survival and the success of your hunting, it's best to travel light. A bologna sandwich and an extra pair of dry socks will serve most of our hunting endeavors much better than would many of the contrivances that are advertised as being "essential."

For Use in the Field

In the field, the items that are really essential for the proper care and treatment of a fallen deer are a knife, a length of nylon cord, and a plastic bag. That is the total list of tools required for field dressing and transporting the deer carcass to the road.

Which knife is best for field dressing a deer? Well, whatever you've got is probably good enough, assuming that the blade is sharp. I have seen deer completely and nicely gutted with no more than a small folding pocket knife, and I have observed on other occasions some rather awkward attempts to perform that same simple task using knives so large that they could have been used to chop firewood. Probably the best choice is a four or five-inch blade of good cutting steel. Such a knife is small enough for the delicate cuts required during certain stages of the field dressing operation, yet is sufficiently sturdy for splitting the sternum of the rib cage. Many deer hunters prefer to also split the pelvis during gutting, and a larger than usual knife is often necessary for this task. However, splitting the pelvis unduly exposes the round steaks to dirt and debris during dragging, so it is best to postpone splitting until it can be easily done with a hatchet or a saw back at the roadside.

Mature buck deer come equipped with seemingly convenient handles called antlers. Nevertheless, dragging a buck out of the woods solely by the antlers usually becomes something less than good fun after the first hundred yards or so. There always seems to be a sharp tine just where you could otherwise grip the main beam for best leverage. A rope can make dragging much easier if you tie the deer's front legs alongside the neck and then extend the same rope from the antlers for towing. Tie a sturdy stick crosswise to your end of the tow rope; this provides a good grip. For many years, I used a length of drapery drawstring that I had scrounged from a rubbish heap. (Talk about a class act!) Finally, after I had knotted the cord in a dozen places, I upgraded to a ten-foot length of quarter-inch nylon rope. This coils up neatly in my pocket yet is more than adequate for the purpose of towing a deer carcass towards the supper table. Nylon ropes tend to fray at each end, so fuse these loose strands together by melting them over a match flame. But be careful; the gooey stuff that forms stays very hot and sticky for a half minute or so.

In third place on the list of absolute essentials is a plastic bag that is large enough to tote the deer's liver, heart, and other exotic goodies that you have rescued from the carcass. The commercial eight- and thirteen-gallon trash bags are somewhat larger than necessary for this particular job, but they also serve admirably as temporary sitting surfaces on soggy days. I know one fellow who does virtually all his deer hunting while perched comfortably upon a trash bag. He carries either the green or brown colored bags early in the season and then switches over to white when the first snowfall appears. Trying to borrow this fellow's bag is like trying to take a blanket away from a two-year-old toddler. (You can get it, but not without a lot of fuss.)

In fact, maintaining possession of one's own plastic bag can require great acting skills. Inevitably, in a group of deer hunters, the first hunter to drop a deer will have neglected to bring a plastic bag. Actually, he never brings one, but he will claim to have forgotten it on this particular day. Shortly, he will say, "Hey, lemme borrow your bag." This is your signal to begin evasive maneuvers. Suddenly begin staring over his shoulder into the forest. Whisper "Shhh . . .". Then, say, "Wow, you should've seen the rack on that buck!" Grab your gun and wildly race off in the direction of the mystery deer. With luck, this tactic will not only save your plastic bag but will also get you excused from the chore of helping drag this fellow's deer out of the woods. And later, you can sneak back and steal the liver that he probably decided to leave behind.

Tools for Skinning and Butchering

First, of course, you need a place to work, a place where the deer can be hung for skinning and the first stages of butchering. On a temporary basis, this can simply be located under a sturdy branch of a backyard tree, as long as the branch is at least seven feet off the ground. Better yet, use the garage or some other enclosed structure where the hanging carcass can be protected from direct sunlight and blowing winds. If you can't find a stout beam that a rope can be thrown over, then plan on installing a couple of large "U" bolts or size "O" threaded ceiling hooks to one of the ceiling joists. Get this chore done long before the deer season opens. Maybe it will bring you good luck, and if it doesn't, there's always next year.

Stringing up a deer is usually a two-person job requiring strength, physical coordination, patience, and in the case of a hunter-and-spouse team, a good marriage — that is, unless you have acquired a block and tackle, which is really the best way to go for hoisting a deer up into skinning position. It is, admittedly, a luxury, but so is indoor plumbing.

Once aloft, the deer should be tightly secured into position with a hemp rope that is at least half an inch in diameter. Nylon rope can be substituted in a pinch, but it tends towards elasticity, which causes the deer to bounce during the pulls and tugs of skinning. Hemp rope, on the other hand, provides a static resistance against which you can exert a steady pull during skinning without the extra fun and games. Remember, use a good strong rope, a half-inch or better. I once had a lesser rope break just as I was working the hide past the last stages of skinning. Luckily, the carcass missed me on its way to the floor, but I had to spend the next half hour picking barn floor debris off the bare carcass. (Note: Use vinegar and a damp cloth to wipe away the hair and other matter that gets stuck onto a freshly skinned carcass.)

The butchering technique described in this book is a two-stage process in which the first stage consists of quartering the carcass into smaller, more easily handled sections. These are the two shoulders, the two haunches, and the neck and torso (more about this later). Finding a place to temporarily store these huge chunks of meat and bone until you proceed to the second stage of butchering can be a problem — that is, it is a problem unless you already have driven a few tenpenny nails in a convenient location on which to hang the sections. This little chore should be done long before you need it done. Don't wait until you have to hold a twenty-pound haunch in one hand while you swing the hammer with the other hand. ("Honey, hold the nail steady, will ya?")

The second stage of butchering involves cutting the meat off the

Fig. 3. A block-and-tackle will reduce the work required for hoisting a deer for skinning. Use hemp rope, which doesn't stretch.

bone, slicing steaks, trimming off the tallow, dicing the stew meat, and rolling the roasts. Most people prefer to perform this job in the warmth of the kitchen, but if you do all this cutting work on the bare kitchen table, you're asking for trouble; the surface will soon be marred and scratched. Old newspapers won't work either; they stick to fresh meat like wallpaper, and you would be reading portions of the classified ads on your supper for months to come. The best bet is to have a portable cutting board, a four-by-four foot section of exterior grade plywood at least half an inch thick. Sand the splinters off the edges and round off the corners. The board will provide ample work space atop a table, and it will withstand the most vigorous cutting. No chopping or hacking is required in venison butchering because all the meat can (and should) be removed by cutting it away from the bone before the "chops" are sliced. When there is no bone to contend with, you don't need a cleaver. The cutting board should be washed after use with soap and hot water and then be stored where the board won't warp or get used inadvertently in a carpentry project.

Every autumn, particularly during the deer season, there is a run on freezer paper. Stores are usually temporarily sold out of it by the third week in November. Get yours while the supply lasts— about the same time you buy a hunting license. Look for freezer paper coated with polyethylene; it does a better job of holding in

Fig. 4. Home butchering requires only a minimum of tools.

moisture. Wrap with the coated side towards the meat. You will need about seventy-five square feet of freezer paper for the average deer if you cut a lot of steaks and make them up into small serving portions. Don't forget masking tape for holding the wrapped packages intact. Use a soft felt tip pen for marking the packages; you don't want to poke any holes in the paper.

Why Commercial Butchers Have Tools You Don't Need

Any newcomer to do-it-yourself venison butchering is apt to be initially intimidated by a quick glance past the meat counter in a commercial butcher's shop. An array of cleavers, chopping blocks, various knives, hand saws, band saws and other sinister looking devices can be viewed there. The display is enough to discourage the average neophyte into believing that his venison butchering will be woefully inadequate from lack of proper equipment. However, that just isn't true. Commercial butchers need all this heavy duty equipment to be able to cut through bone. That's plain and simple; the techniques for butchering domestic animals require power tools and massive cleavers for the cutting and chopping of bone. But venison butchering can easily be done with far fewer tools because the meat can (and should) be removed from the skeletal structure *before* the final cuttings are made. It is easily possible to use the same hunting knife for the total rendering of a deer from field dressing through skinning and quartering to final butchering. This is no exaggeration; a five-inch blade knife of good cutting steel is the minimum equipment required for venison butchering. Admittedly, there are two or three other household tools that will make the job easier (and these will soon be described), but even these are mere toys compared to the savage contrivances on display in a commercial butcher's shop. Rest easy: the Indians were able to butcher a deer with no more than a sharpened rock. Of course, the women did all the work, but that shouldn't make much of a difference.

Probably the best contribution of modern technology to home butchering has been the electric knife. While it is certainly possible to cope without one, an electric knife greatly aids in the straight-and-true slicing of steaks. For uniform cooking, a steak should be of uniform thickness. You don't want one edge of a steak to be over-cooked while the other edge is undercooked. An electric knife is your

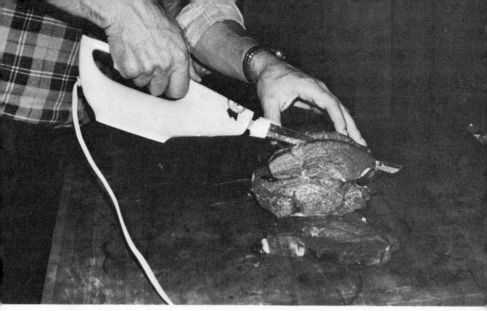

Fig. 5. An electric knife helps produce more even thickness when cutting venison steaks.

best bet for accurate and consistent thicknesses of cuts. In a pinch, substitute a long carving knife having a blade of at least eight inches.

Whichever knife or knives you use, and for whatever purposes, a sharp blade makes any cutting job a lot easier, even safer. (But you already knew that.) Actually, although skinning a deer gets off to a faster start with a nicely sharpened knife, the main work in skinning consists more of pulling and tugging than it does of cutting. In fact, a dull knife is conveniently less apt to nick the hide during those occasional cuts through fat and tissue that adhere to the inner surface of the hide. Butchering, however, is a different situation. For butchering, you want the knife to be as sharp as the proverbial razor. Settle for any less than that and butchering will become a chore instead of an interesting pastime. Time spent stepping aside from butchering to sharpen a knife is not wasted; sharpening is a shortcut that helps get the job done faster. If you don't sharpen a butchering knife at least half a dozen times between start and finish, you're cutting with a dull knife much of the time. Use either a whetstone or a sharpening steel to keep the blade edge in good, sharp condition. In the final stages of sharpening a blade, push, don't pull, the edge over the sharpener. This action helps prevent a microscopic buildup of feathered steel on the cutting edge. At best, there may

Fig. 6. Using a knife sharpener will save you time and effort in the long run.

still be a curling of steel biased to one side or the other of the cutting edge, which bends over at the first cut. This curling is too small to be seen with the naked eye, but you can check for it by sliding a thumb across the flat of the blade towards the edge. If a small ridge can be felt, more on one side than the other, lightly swipe that side of the blade across the sharpener one more time to bend that ridge back into alignment. This will give you a cutting edge that will make venison cut like warm butter.

Another tool that aids in butchering is a saw. I don't mean a meat saw or a band saw, just virtually any saw that might happen to be on your workbench, that's all. The only sawing that is required in boneless venison butchering is about a twelve-inch cut to split the spine from the tail bone to just above the hips. This separates the two haunches so that each can later be handled more easily. The quality of adjacent venison is unaffected by this minor sawing because none of it actually comes in contact with the bone chips that are produced. I use an ordinary carpenter's crosscut saw and then wash it off afterwards. A saw will also come in handy for cutting off the lower legs prior to skinning, but even this can be done with a few deft knife cuts around the lowest joint.

Venison butchering can be made into a difficult and prolonged chore, or it can be done as an interesting and fairly easy project.

Ironically, the simplest method, employing boneless butchering techniques, requires the fewest tools, ones that most hunters already own.

Where to Get Tools and Chemicals for Taxidermy and Tanning

Beyond the point when the last wrapped package of venison is placed in the freezer, there still exists a whole new world of ways in which a deer carcass can be even further utilized. Now we are looking at hide tanning, leathercraft, amateur taxidermy, and handicrafts such as making antler knife handles, antler buttons, and antler trophy mounts. The full scope of these pastimes is limited only by our imagination, good taste, and of course, the availability of tools and chemicals. Probably the single greatest obstacle to any "do-it-yourself" venture is the faulty assumption that something we don't yet know how to do is more complicated than it really is. While it is certainly true that the right tool used in the right plan can save a lot of time, it is also true that we can usually make do with lesser substitutes, particularly if we are going to do the job only once and have time to spare.

Of all the hunting-related crafts, taxidermy probably has the greatest aura of mystery about it. Taxidermists are often held in awe by the hunting public; we figure that their skills fall somewhere in between alchemy and surgery. Actually, most mounts are rather simply done. Beauty is only skin-deep, and that is the beauty of taxidermy. Most deer mounts consist of no more than a preserved skin draped and sewn over a lifelike form with glass eyes and earliners. The real art of taxidermy is in the finishing touches—the making sure that the artificial form is filled out under the skin in a lifelike way, the positioning of the features, and lastly, the application of black paint to nose and eye ducts to make them appear moist and lifelike. That is taxidermy. Yes, it is an art, but not one that would be beyond the capability of any person with skilled hands, an eye for realism, and a little patience.

There still remain questions regarding tools and equipment: what is needed, and where can they be obtained? The full requirements of tools, forms, and chemicals are covered in detail in later chapters. All of these items can be obtained through the mail via the catalogs of several supply houses which service the taxidermy industry. The addresses of these supply houses can usually be found in the classified advertisements of most major outdoor magazines, or you can go straight to a local taxidermist and perhaps get what you need right there. It may seem a little presumptuous to ask a taxidermist to supply you with taxidermy equipment, but I have encountered a surprising degree of cooperation in doing this. (Perhaps the reason for this cooperation is that one of the very best advertisements for professional taxidermy is a poorly done amateur mount!) The cost of buying taxidermy supplies this way will be higher than catalog prices, but the convenience is worth it. Of course, if a taxidermist's own inventory of supplies is running on the low side, he or she is not going to sell you anything off the shelf. Make your acquaintance and requests early. Send for mail-order catalogs later if you run up against a brick wall using the personal approach.

There are many specialty tools that can be acquired right at home. For example, one of the best tools obtainable for removing the tightly adhered skin from around the base of a buck's antlers is a common screwdriver. A meat-carving knife can be modified into a hide-fleshing tool by inserting the tip of the knife into a block of wood which

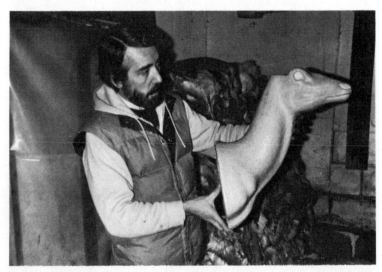

Fig. 7. The beauty of taxidermy is only skin deep. Here the author holds an artificial mounting form, which greatly reduces the work of do-it-yourself taxidermy.

will then serve as the second handle. Sewing thread is sewing thread whether it is used for patching pants or sewing up a full shoulder buck mount. Even the head and neck form can be constructed from papier maché and modeling clay (or using the original skull, boiled and cleaned), but that approach involves a great deal of work. Improvise where you can, but don't stretch ingenuity to the point that the job isn't being done right because the tools are inadequate.

What Your Freezer Should Be Asked to Do

The good news about storing frozen venison is that the trimmed and boned meat from an average deer will seldom require more than one and a half cubic feet of space. Honest: this may not seem possible, but it is true for the vast majority of deer. A very large deer might require all of two cubic feet but no more than that, unless you have not wrapped the packages tightly. Most refrigerator freezers conveniently have sufficient space for the storage of an entire boned deer and can still provide room enough for the frozen orange juice and the ice cube trays (But not much of anything else!). The catch, however, is that the lowest possible temperatures of most refrigerator freezers are inadequate for the long-term storage of meat. Although 32°F. is the freezing point of pure water, the water in venison and other meats contains dissolved minerals and other natural substances which lower the actual freezing point. Additionally, enzyme and certain bacterial action is not frozen, even at 15–25°F. Real deep-freezing doesn't occur until below 0°F, and to achieve those sub-zero temperatures for storage times of several months or more a separate deep freezer is required.

Nevertheless, a refrigerator freezer will adequately preserve venison for two or three months and maybe a little longer than that, if the meat is particularly well-wrapped and the temperature dial is turned as low as possible. At the end of this time, the venison does not necessarily go bad on you; instead, it usually just begins to lose the quality of flavor. There is something else involved here too. Because the temperature in a refrigerator freezer tends to fluctuate more often than in a deep freezer, ice crystals gradually grow larger within the meat until the cellular walls are punctured. This action allows flavor to escape as soon as the meat is thawed, even before it can be cooked.

The solutions to this dilemma, if you don't have access to a deep freeze, are to (1) eat as much of the deer as you can during the first two or three months of storage, or (2) preserve part or all of the deer by canning and smoking.

Canning Equipment

Canning is an excellent method for preserving venison, and not just for the stew meat either! Whole roasts and even burgers can be canned for later enjoyment. Once venison has been canned, there is no need to pour additional energy dollars into keeping it preserved, and when you open a container, the venison is already cooked, needing only to be warmed back up to serving temperatures. It's truly surprising that more people don't use this time-honored method for preserving venison. (See details in chapter 7.)

Venison, like any other meat, and many vegetables, requires special

Fig. 8. For safe and effective meat canning, use a pressure cooker-canner, wide-mouth canning jars, and be sure to follow the instructions.

canning procedures because the acid content is insufficient to counteract bacterial growth. What this means is that venison must be canned using a pressure cooker-canner, not just with an ordinary pressure cooker. You must be able to attain 240°F. for an extended period of time to insure that all bacteria are killed rather than just knocked silly. So, use a pressure cooker-*canner,* which is usually made from cast aluminum with a sealable rim and appropriate gauges.

The boned meat from an entire deer of average size can be stored in about forty quart canning jars. If the steaks and better roasts are kept aside for freezing, and only the stew meat is to be canned, then six to eight quart canning jars will do the job. Use wide-mouth jars for ease of getting the venison in and out of them. Ordinary mayonnaise jars are not suited for high pressure canning.

Equipment for Smoking Venison

First, you go out and chop down about twenty trees, and then . . . no, no, just kidding. You don't have to build a smokehouse. A covered charcoal grill will do the job nearly as well, and a converted junk refrigerator will serve even better (although it won't look as good in your backyard as a genuine log smokehouse). Even a large cardboard box works well for meat smoking because only the wood embers get hot enough to smolder in a proper smoking setup. You don't cook the meat, you preserve it. Meat preservation occurs as a result of smoking because combustion chemicals from the smoke become dissolved in the meat tissues. These chemicals greatly retard the growth of molds and bacteria while contributing a smoky flavor.

You will need wood chips or sawdust from an aromatic hardwood (such as hickory, oak, apple, cherry, etc.), and you might want to add certain spices or herbs to the wood in small amounts for added flavors. A metal pan will serve as a container and combustion chamber. Venison is prepared for smoking by being soaked overnight in a brine solution. Table salt will introduce an iodine flavor, so use any other low-cost salt such as rock or dairy salt. Use crockery, plastic, or stainless steel for holding the brine solution. That's about it. You can follow either the fancy or the plain-and-simple route towards success in smoking venison. Either way, the end results are worth the effort . . . makes me hungry just to think about it.

Chapter 3

Field Dressing

The End Is the Beginning

The deer is down. This time you won and the buck lost. In order to claim your total prize, however, there is a simple chore that has to be performed first. The deer must be field dressed as soon as possible so that the venison can be quickly cooled to preserve the quality of flavor and to retard the spread of bacteria within the abdominal cavity.

Calculating Live Weights

Gutting a deer also lessens the burden when you later drag the carcass back to civilization. In fact, a gutted buck weighs (on the average) only 79 percent of the original on-the-hoof weight. For a doe, the dressed yield is 78 percent. These numbers are accurate within one or two percent for the vast majority of deer and were obtained several years ago by the New York State Department of Conservation during an extensive survey and study of the deer herd. Later, if you weigh the dressed deer, you can calculate the live weight by dividing the hanging weight by 0.79 for a buck and 0.78 for a doe. But for right now, let's get that deer field dressed.

Make Sure the Deer Is Dead

A fallen deer should be approached very cautiously, even if it appears to be as dead as a stone. If the deer's eyes are closed, that's almost a sure sign that the deer actually is still *alive.* There are many hair-raising and not-so-funny tales about close encounters occurring between unsuspecting hunters and "dead" deer that suddenly came to life. Shoot again if there is even the faintest sign of life; aim for the heart or the base of the neck. Finally, test the deer by touching an eye with a branch or the muzzle of your gun. If there is no reaction, no blinking, then you can proceed with field dressing. Remember to unload your gun first. This would also be a good time to fill out your tag (if that's required by local game laws) before getting involved up to your elbows in field dressing.

Bleeding and Removing Metatarsal Glands

It used to be a very common practice to first cut a deer's throat, the thinking being that the meat would be improved if the carcass was "bled." This concept originated with commercial and down-on-the-farm butchering practices, where chickens, pigs, and other domestic animals are dispatched with a deft cut that produces fast bleeding as the heart pumps its final rhythms. However, a dead deer's heart has already stopped, and no significant bleeding can later take place. If the deer's heart is still beating, you have absolutely no business messing around down by the throat amidst those potentially lethal antlers and hooves. Today's modern rifle bullets and shotgun slugs do sufficient damage so that a deer, in most cases, has already bled internally by the time you arrive on the scene. Also, if there is a chance that you might want to have the deer mounted as a trophy, remember that no amount of skilled taxidermy work can repair the cut hairs and jagged outline of a sliced throat. Go ahead and do it if you want to, but "sticking" a deer isn't really necessary.

The same thing applies to the removal of the metatarsal glands that are located on the inside of the rear legs, between the hoof and the first joint. These glands appear as elongated dark brown tufts of hair, and they secrete a noxious-smelling musk during the rut. Leave these beauties alone; they stink and can foul the taste of any portion of meat that the secretions touch. If you cut away the metatarsal glands, your knife becomes contaminated, and the disturbed glands can ooze at the cut ends . . . which reminds me of a day in my boyhood when I had brought home a dead skunk from my trapline and had begun skinning it on the picnic table in the backyard. My mother peeked out the back door and said, "Are you really *sure* you want to do that?" After a while, I wasn't.

Of course, some hunters, particularly those who hunt with bow and arrow, remove the metatarsal glands for use as deer scent the following year. The glands are first dried prior to being stored in a sealed glass jar, and then when the next deer season rolls around, the glands can be reactivated by adding a little moisture. Pinned to a trouser leg or attached to a tree stand, these glands help mask human odors. If you decide to keep your deer's glands, remove them *after* the rest of the field dressing has been completed.

Why the Rush?

There are several different ways to do the actual job of field dressing a deer, at least in the beginning stages. Nevertheless, the end product is a deer carcass from which the intestines, lungs, and other internal organs have been removed. The whole job can appear very complicated to a beginner, seeming to fall at a skill level somewhere between an appendectomy and a heart transplant. Actually, there is more margin for error than many veteran hunters would lead you to believe. Properly field dressing a deer is really no more difficult than changing a tire.

Field dressing is merely unzipping the deer down the front and emptying out the entrails, much the same as you would clean out a rabbit or squirrel, but of course on a somewhat grander scale. Care should be taken that the contents of the bladder and large intestine do not spill out upon the meat, but even if this accident does occur, the carcass can certainly be salvaged by simply washing it off afterwards. Even a botched-up field dressing job will leave the venison in better condition than if the deer were left unattended for several hours. You want the carcass to cool as rapidly as possible, and field dressing helps achieve this goal by exposing more of the venison to the cool air. Cooling deters the growth of bacteria that begins culturing around the wound area and in the intestines as soon as the deer's natural resistances have stopped functioning. So, jump in there and get that deer gutted right now. (We've wasted enough time standing around here just talking about it.)

Step 1: The Four Basic Beginning Methods

The most complicated chore of field dressing a deer begins right here in the first step, and it concerns the removal of the bladder and the colon. There are four basically different ways to accomplish this goal, and whichever of these ways that you decide to use will determine your first action.

The *ream-and-tie method* requires a deep cut all the way around the anus. Insert the knife about four inches deep so that you are cutting the colon free of the fatty tissues that hold it. When the colon is free, pull the anus (with a bit of hide still attached) far enough out of the carcass so you can tie it shut with a piece of twine. Later, when the abdominal cavity has been opened, you will be able to pull the colon and anus into the cavity for dumping with the rest of the entrails. Tying the anus prevents the spillage of offal onto the carcass. This method leaves the bladder for removal in Step 2.

The split-and-strip method involves splitting the pelvis bone to expose the full length of the colon and the urethra of the reproductive organ, which is connected internally to the bladder. These can then be stripped from the carcass. This technique, however, is not applied until after the abdominal wall has been opened in Step 2. This means that you can delay the inevitable for at least a little while longer. It also means that your first action will be to open the abdominal wall.

Splitting the pelvic bone works almost like magic if you get the right spot. Otherwise, it's as difficult as trying to open a clamshell with a wooden spoon. When the abdominal cut has been extended down through the crotch, the broad width of the pelvic bone is exposed. It has a "seam" where the two sides connect in the middle. Place the sharp edge of your knife against this seam and then place the heel of your free hand on top of the knife and exert a hardy shove. If the knife placement is perfect, the pelvic bone will pop open.

Fig. 9. The "ream-and-tie" method requires a deep cut all the way around the anus to free it from the fatty tissues of the pelvis. Pull part way out and tie shut with a piece of string.

You might have to try using the knife instead as a pry bar, inserted vertically into the seam. But be careful: many good knives have been ruined in this manner. A hand axe or bone saw will do the job if all other efforts fail.

The *all-in-one pull method* requires a little more skill and practice than the other methods, but it permits you to remove the genitals, colon, and bladder all in one fell swoop with the least risk of spillage. Here's how it's done.

A cut through the skin parallel to the reproductive organ is extended all the way to the anus. This permits the underlying tube, with scrotum attached, to be freed its full length along the crotch and backside of the deer. You will then see that this tube enters the body cavity next to the colon. With the freed tube lying outstretched from the deer, make a deep cut that circumscribes both the colon and the reproductive tube together. This cut is made in very similar fashion to the one described in the "ream-and-tie method," but here the cut includes the reproductive tube also. Later, when you have opened the abdomen and are ready to dump the entrails, the reproductive tube and colon can be pulled right into the body cavity. The bladder requires no special care, as it will fall free with all the other entrails.

The *quick-and-dirty method* is used a lot more often than many hunters will admit. It's merely cutting off the large intestine from inside, near the exit, after the deer's abdomen has been opened. The advantage of this method is that, at least, the deer has been gutted so the meat can begin cooling. And, as we said earlier, poorly done field dressing is far better than no field dressing at all. The drawback to being quick and dirty is that, although the job is quick, the venison gets dirty. The unremoved colon, about six inches long, stores a large quantity of deer "pellets" that will begin slipping into the body cavity

Fig. 10. The "all-in-one-pull" method involves trimming the reproductive tube and scrotum away from the crotch so that they later can be pulled inside the abdominal cavity through the anus. This method is complicated, but it results in least spillage of urine and offal.

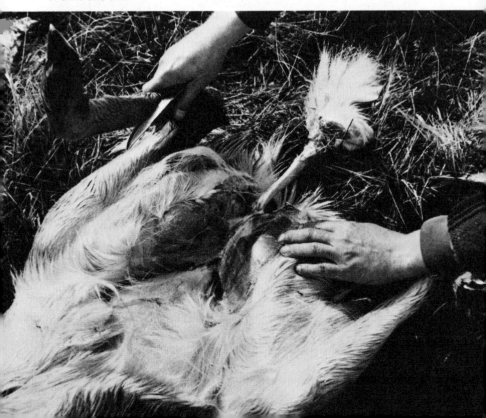

where they will soon sour the meat. Let's take a step back for a moment. If the colon is tied off with string or a twist-tie, the large intestine can then be cut without much spillage. Similarly, the bladder can be tied off on both the inlet and outlet tubes before it is removed. Later, when you're back home, back at the ranch, back at camp, or back at the roadside (pick one, any one), then you *must* split the pelvis or ream the colon in order to remove the pellets.

That's it — the four basic techniques for beginning the field dressing. The best one is the one that *you* can do the best. Uncle Harry probably does it differently than Grandpa, and old Fred-down-the-road probably swears by an even different method. As long as the venison is properly cooled and protected from contamination, it doesn't matter which technique is used to get started.

Step 2: The Two Basic Finishing Methods

This is the step where you unzip the belly of the deer to expose the intestines and other internal organs. With the deer on its back on reasonably level ground, make a shallow starting cut into the hide only, at the lower tip of the chest where the ribs begin. This is the sternum, or breastbone. You could start at the other end, near the crotch, but the sternum rides higher above the intestines when the deer is on its back and there is less risk of making too deep a puncture. With the knife positioned sharp edge *up,* and guided by two fingers on either side of the blade, split the belly skin all the way to the crotch. This will expose the abdominal wall. Make this same long cut again, this time opening the abdominal wall. Be careful that you don't also cut into the intestines. Unless the deer has been gut-shot, the now exposed abdominal cavity will be virtually bloodless.

Once again, there exists more than one technique by which the intestines and organs can be removed. The *two-stage gutting method* involves an extra turning of the deer onto its belly for the first dumping, but this method also provides more working space and is more appropriate for handling the messy interior of a gut-shot deer. First tilt the deer slightly on one side and probe with a hand inserted around the outside of the mass of innards to locate any connections with the abdominal cavity walls. Cut the liver and kidneys away from their attachments near the spine. Then tilt the deer to its other side and repeat this process until all hidden connections (*except* the colon

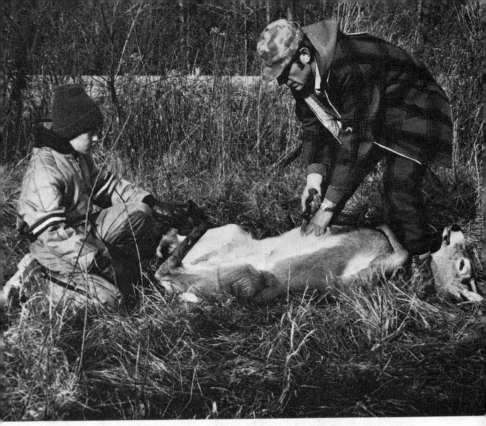

Fig. 11. Start the belly incision at the sternum (the "breastbone") of the rib cage. At this location, the intestines have dropped below the abdominal wall, and there is less risk of puncturing them. Young Scott Thayer is about to learn from his Uncle John how to field dress a deer.

and bladder) are severed. Then, after this, proceed with whichever method you elected to use in Step 1 to solve the problem of the colon, bladder, and reproductive organ. This means that, at this point, you will either pull them into the cavity, tie them off, or split the pelvis.

Okay, having done that, now grasp the tube (the gullet) that leads into the top end of the stomach and cut it off just below the lungs. Now you're ready for the first dumping. Roll the deer over onto its stomach, grab hold of both hind feet, and lift the deer up and away from the gut pile. Don't quit now; the job is only half done because the lungs, heart and windpipe need to be removed. With the deer once again on its back, cut along the circumference of the diaphragm. This is a thin membrane that extends like the stretched skin on a drum to separate the lungs from the stomach and other lower organs. After the diaphragm is removed, reach up inside the rib cage, past the lungs, until you can grasp the windpipe. Cut this loose and the entire package of heart and lungs will fall free and can be dumped. The preceding description of cutting the windpipe is the method you should definitely use if there is any chance that the deer will be mounted as a trophy. The taxidermist will need to use most of the hide that extends around the shoulders and chest to achieve a hand-some mount. If the deer will not be mounted, you can instead open the rib cage for easier access to the windpipe. This can be done by splitting the sternum. Stand straddling the deer's chest, facing the head, and place the knife blade slightly to one side of the sternum. With a two-fisted grip on the knife and a sturdy, outward heave-ho,

Fig. 12. Split the sternum with a knife, which gives access to the diaphragm, as shown in the photo. Standing on the deer's hind legs will help keep the carcass stable.

the rib-cage can be split up the middle all the way to the base of the throat. Doing this also enhances the cooling rate of the carcass.

Now, let's go back and take a look at how the *one-step gutting method* is done. You might like this method better, particularly if you have made a one-shot kill in the upper body. The sequence of chores is the same as in the two-stage method, *except* that you don't cut the stomach gullet and you don't do any dumping until the very end. Doing it this way has the drawback of making the cutting of the diaphragm more difficult because you won't be able to see all of it at one time, but the overall gutting is less apt to be messy by going this route.

Special Treatment for the Tenderloins, Heart, and Liver

After the deer has been completely gutted, prop it belly-side down to aid in drainage. Unless spillage of feces, urine, or stomach contents has occurred, it is best to not wash or wipe out the interior. Water promotes the spreading of bacteria, and the dry leaves or grass that you would use for wiping out the interior would only make a terrible mess. Your best bet is to let the interior drain and then air dry. Prop the chest cavity open with a stick to promote these actions. If flies, yellow jackets and other pesky little flying critters seem to want to make a meal out of the deer, you can discourage them with a liberal coating of black pepper. Sprinkle the pepper throughout the abdominal cavity; it will form a protective casing on the bare meat and will also retard spoilage from bacterial action.

The tenderloins will best retain their toothsome flavor if they are removed immediately after the field dressing is finished. Many hunters neglect to do this, and the tenderloins subsequently acquire an off-taste from having been in contact with the blood and debris of field dressing. The tenderloins are two elongated muscles that are attached to either side of the spine in the lower back region. You can see them exposed to the inside of the abdominal cavity. Removal is easy—just slip your hand in behind them, one at a time, and pull. Sometimes a knife cut at the attached ends will help. Full details on the removal of the tenderloins are given in chapter 6.

By all means, don't forget to rescue the heart and liver from the gut pile. Along with the tenderloins, these portions of meat are the ones most often selected for the traditional celebration supper. After a long, hard (but successful!) day afield, a roasted heart filled with stuffing, or a platter of bacon-fried liver and onions, will be just what the hungry hunter needs to round out the day on a perfect note.

The heart comes from the deer encased in a tough, thin membrane that will protect the meat from dust and dirt. You might as well leave this membrane on until the heart is prepared for cooking. The liver, unfortunately, doesn't come from nature in the same convenient packaging and should instead be plopped into a plastic bag. As soon as possible, wash the liver in fresh water; in fact, soak the liver in water if you can. Liver will acquire an off-taste faster than any other portion of meat from a deer carcass, so it should quickly meet its destiny with either a hot fry pan or a cold freezer. By the way, you might have read or heard elsewhere that the gall bladder should first be removed from the liver. The explanation usually offered is that the bile will ruin the meat. Well, yes, it probably could, except that deer *don't have* gall bladders! Most other mammals have gall bladders, but deer, being ruminants that forage on a high cellulose-low fat diet, don't need those bitter little things for food digestion. So, you can forget about the gall bladder—there isn't one.

Speaking about forgetting, if you neglected to bring along a plastic bag, you can still carry the heart and liver out of the woods impaled on a forked stick. Cut a branched twig just below the "Y" and then cut one of the protruding branches short to form something like an "L." In this way, a little hook will be formed at the bottom end of your handy carrier to prevent the heart and liver from slipping off after the long end of the stick has been poked through them.

Why Discard the Kidneys, Tripe, and Casings?

There are two other organs that most American hunters seem inclined to leave for the crows and 'possums. These are the kidneys and the stomach—or rather, the lining of the stomach, which is called "tripe." I have not, frankly, ever eaten the venison version of these two items, but I have enjoyed the beef versions on many occasions served in spiced, hot meat pies. These meals took place in Australia, which is a meat-rich country that could afford, like we think we can, to discard these internal organs. But they don't, and maybe we shouldn't either. However, venison kidneys are embedded in a thick, fatty tallow that must be removed before cooking.

If you plan to make your own link venison sausage, then it would be wise to consider salvaging some of the deer's small intestine for use as a casing. Otherwise, you're going to have to later purchase sheep intestine. Might as well stick with venison all the way—it's a genuine, natural product of nature.

Chapter 4

Transporting from Forest to Home

Why Always Uphill?

Hauling a deer from the site of the kill back towards civilization is a chore that we, as hunters, don't really mind. Somehow, a sense of ownership is attained as we pass through the gauntlet of obstacles that nature places along our pathway. There is no such thing as a typical situation to describe the problems involved in transporting a deer. The deer might have been dropped on a wooded Pennsylvania mountainside, in the Texas hill country, deep in a Florida swamp, a Colorado valley, or way back in the piney woods of Michigan. There are so many different possibilities, each of which demands special logistics for transporting the venison from the woods to the supper table. But regardless where you hunt, there is one fact, one common factor shared by all successful deer hunters, which is this: the way back is always uphill, you can bet on it.

I've heard some stories that run contrary to that theory. One fellow, whose name is omitted here because I can't vouch for his honesty, tells the story (at least once every deer season) about the time he shot a buck within a hundred yards of the roadside after having trailed it on snow for several hours. The deer, so the story goes, ran up to this fellow's parked car and expired on the spot. Another tale involves a man who was hunting in unfamiliar territory. He got lost, and during his aimless wanderings a fine buck jumped out of the underbrush. The lost hunter shot the deer, gutted and tagged it, and then proceeded on without the deer to first find the way home. Two other hunters who were out looking for him discovered the deer instead, so they towed it out of the woods, where they met our lucky friend at the roadside drinking coffee.

Don't plan on having this kind of luck the next time you are faced with the ordeal of transporting a deer. Plan instead on the worst circumstances because that's usually the way these things work. There are, of course, a few things you can do to make the job a little easier.

Conventional and Improved Dragging Methods

The most conventional means of moving a deer carcass is to drag it along the ground; that is, one or two hunters grab the deer by the antlers and simply start walking. Sounds easy, but it isn't. Deer have the ability to gain weight while being dragged in this fashion, and their antlers have the mysterious power to curve around and poke you in the wrist on every other step. The Olympic decathlon would be more representative of human athletic endeavor if one of the events included bare-handed deer hauling. There's something strange about the weight distribution of a deer carcass that causes it to slide sideways if pulled by the antlers. Also, because hunters' arms are connected at the shoulder, a deer towed by the antlers has to be pulled *up* at the same time it is being pulled *out*. There's an easy way around this dilemma, and all it involves is a ten-foot length of quarter-inch nylon rope and about a minute or so of your time. And by the way, this little trick also works for doe, which many successful hunters have discovered (to their chagrin) don't even have antlers for handles.

Using the rope, tie the deer's front legs either alongside, or atop, the deer's head. This will prevent the legs from catching on obstacles and will also help prevent the deer carcass from steering sideways as you pull. Then extend the rope around the head so that legs and head can be tied and held snugly together. Now, the loose end of

Fig. 13. Dragging a deer by the antlers is hard work. You have to lift and pull at the same time while the antler tines dig into your arm. This is the "wrong way" to do it, as demonstrated by the author.

the rope, the end you're going to pull on, can either be fastened to your belt or to a hefty stick. The stick provides something that you can grasp for pulling. I have found that tying the stick in its middle permits me to shove both my belly and the crook of one arm into the effort of pulling. Another option is to tie the loose end of the rope to your belt. This works quite decently if the rope is sufficiently long and you are consequently able to pull with the belt riding on the points of your hipbones. If the rope is too short, you'll lose your pants.

There are deer-towing harnesses on the market, designed for placing around your shoulder or waist, and they produce better results than the belt method.

There's another very convenient method for dragging a deer, but it's one that very few outdoor writers ever mention because, well, it simply looks so amateurish. But it works, particularly on snow-covered ground. And, lacking a rope, it's virtually the only way that you can tow a doe or a short-antlered spike buck out of the woods. This feat is accomplished by towing the deer backwards, by the hind legs. Obviously, a buck with a large rack would not pull in this manner very easily; you'd plow a furrow deep enough to plant corn. The backwards pull is best done by two hunters, one on each hind leg. Actually, four hunters do an even better job of sharing the load if they can keep out of each other's way. Probably the reason that the backwards drag isn't used more often on small deer is because it seems to go "against the grain" of the direction the hair grows on a deer's back. However, once you start pulling the deer, the hair reverses direction where the deer contacts the ground and causes hardly any resistance at all. As far as potential harm to the hide is concerned, that also is minimal for short hauls. The standing joke about dragging a deer backwards is that, if you pull on the wrong end of the deer, you just end up deeper in the woods. If anyone ever makes fun of you for pulling a deer the "wrong" way, you can shut them up in a hurry by asking them for some help with the load.

Fig. 14. To streamline the carcass for dragging, tie the front legs between the antlers and then loop the rope around the deer's snout for straight-ahead towing.

Fig. 15. With the deer tied and trussed as shown in fig. 14, a buck can be towed more easily. Bill Sheesley demonstrates good form with his 1982 buck.

It has been claimed by some that dragging a deer over rough ground will bruise the venison. I don't believe that, at least not within the scope of normal handling. Of course, throwing a deer carcass off the top of a cliff would not exactly improve the venison, but ordinary dragging is not going to harm the meat. Bruising of venison is negligible under most conditions because of the fact that a field-dressed deer will have lost nearly all of the blood from the veins, arteries, and even the capillaries. In the absence of blood in the carcass, bruising can't occur to any significant extent.

Carrying Deer, or "Macho Muscle Spasms"

Deer can, of course, be physically carried out of the woods. There are several methods by which this can be accomplished and, obviously, the smaller the deer is, the better these methods work. I admire and respect the hunter who is physically able to perform this task with a good-sized buck. But you'll never catch me doing it; I have even more respect for hernias and popped discs. Smaller deer . . . well, that's a different situation. Yearling deer under a hundred pounds can be carried with relative ease if their weight is properly distributed for a one-man carry. That's the trick to carrying deer; get that dead weight bundled up so that it can't swing to a different rhythm than what your footsteps are following.

If a small deer's legs are tied together, the carcass can be slung over a hunter's shoulders in the same way that a fishing creel is carried; that is, the deer's body hangs down by one hip while the legs extend upward and diagonally across the chest. Performed in this way, deer carrying can be made to appear easy, but it is not considered by most hunters to be a form of recreational activity. There are better ways to have fun; this isn't one of them. Neither is the method in which the entire carcass is draped across the back of both shoulders, with the deer's legs grasped in the hunter's arms. This technique is also rather messy because the gutted deer is positioned so that the open abdomen rests upon the carrier's shoulders.

A major drawback to any of the one-man carrying methods is that rest breaks are not easily obtained. First you have to put the deer down. That's the easy part; picking it back up again is a different matter. Lifting dead weight is far different, and far more awkward, than lifting barbells or furniture. Another drawback is that a carried deer absolutely must be draped with fluorescent orange, or be disguised in other ways, so that under no circumstances could another hunter mistake your cargo for a live deer. 'Nuff said?

The Pole Carry

The two-man pole carry method has certain advantages in that the deer's weight can be shared and that the entire burden can be set down and lifted up more easily for rest breaks. Several hunting buddies and I tried the pole carry method a couple of years ago with a medium sized buck that one of us had shot down behind my rural home. Having had this experience, I won't claim that pole carrying is the answer to the deer transporting dilemma. We discovered certain disadvantages. First, in order to obtain a pole that was both sufficiently long and sturdy enough to hoist a deer, we had to cut a maple sapling that was nearly five inches in diameter at the thickest end. This sapling, which was actually a minor tree, probably contributed in the ballpark of about thirty pounds of weight to our total burden. We laid the buck on its back, placed the pole along the abdomen, and tied each pair of the deer's legs so that they snugly straddled the pole. We also made sure that the deer's midriff and head were secured closely to the pole with rope so the carcass would not swing while we walked. As soon as the first two men lifted our neatly tied burden, they realized that this wasn't going to be fun. The rest of us trailed along behind, carrying the guns and making wisecracks at the expense of our two laboring fellows. ("Weaklings!" "Clumsy oafs!") Then, when it was our turn to carry, we received the same treatment. The load was surprisingly heavy and awkward to maneuver through the brush and briars. Because the deer obstructed the view of the man bringing up the rear, he couldn't keep in step with the man in front and consequently would inadvertently push or tug at the pole as both men tried to navigate forward. We also attempted putting two men on both ends of the pole to share the load, but this made matters even more awkward than before. For one thing, no two of us were exactly the same height. We finally got the deer back to my house, but we all avowed that our feat had been a one-time event. We might have had better success by using two poles, one on either side of the deer, so the burden could have been more uniformly shared by four carriers. However, that approach would have added another thirty pounds or more. There also would have been the problem of maneuvering too wide a load through the closely-grown woodlands. So, no thanks: the pole carry method looks good in pictures, but it really isn't a better way to haul deer through wooded regions. It certainly is a viable alternative on open, flat ground where the walking is easier. But, in that kind of territory, where are you going to find the right kind of tree to cut down?

Field Quartering

Probably the easiest way to transport a deer for long distances over rough terrain is to pack it out in either rough-cut sections or in the form of boned meat. This is not as difficult or as complicated as it might seem. However, in most parts of the country, there seems to exist a certain reluctance to bring anything less than a whole deer home from the hunting grounds. Apparently, the sight of a complete deer hanging on display provides part of the overall enjoyment of the hunt for many of us. We hesitate to mar the appearance of our personal trophy too quickly; we prefer that there be a time for appreciation in between the kill and the consumption. Okay, I'll buy that. But certainly there also are tough situations now and then when, let's face it, the overall hunting experience would be a lot sweeter if we didn't have to wrestle a whole deer carcass over miles of uphill dragging.

The simplest way to lessen the total burden is to cut the deer in half, just above the hips. This is no big deal; it can be done in less than a minute using no more than a hunting knife, after the deer has been gutted. Simply cut through the flanks and across the lower back until only the spine keeps the two halves intact at the waist. Then grasp the hind legs and twist; the carcass will snap into two sections, fore and aft. The hind quarters can then be carried piggy-back style (on your shoulders), and the front section can later be dragged out with relative ease. Cutting the deer in half ruins the usefulness of the hide for many of the larger garments that could be made from it and totally destroys its sale value. You can, however, save the entire hide by partially skinning the deer before cutting the carcass in half. To do this, skin up the hindquarters to just past the hips. First, cut an "inseam" on the inner side of each hind leg and then peel the skin off the legs and up over the rump. (See chapter 5 for more complete details.) A freshly-killed warm deer carcass is very easy to skin, and this little hindquarter skinning chore probably won't require more than five minutes of your time. It results, however, with the hindquarters being exposed as bare venison, which now has no protection from dirt, dry leaves, and other bits of matter that will adhere to the sticky flesh. A convenient carrying handle for the hindquarters can be devised by inserting a sturdy stick through both hocks. Make a slit behind each Achilles tendon for this purpose. With the one stick supporting both legs, you can lift the hindquarters by grasping the stick. Prop the stick horizontally over one shoulder and you're ready to do some fairly easy and comfortable transporting. Either make a return trip for the other half, or con a buddy into towing it out for you. A hiker's pack frame provides,

of course, a better method for hauling portions of a deer because it is designed to spread the weight of the cargo over your back and shoulders.

Spoilage Enroute Home

Sometimes, under certain circumstances, the job of transporting venison can be made easier in the long run by first completely boning the deer while still in the woods. I have never done it this way, but I can see boning as a credible alternative for the hunter who backpacks many miles into the wilderness. In fact, the boneless butchering techniques described in chapter 7 would apply very well to field butchering. The haunch and rump meat, the backstrap sirloins, and the shoulder muscle and neck fillets would, if trimmed from the skeletal structure, weigh only about sixty percent of the total carcass weight. The hide would add approximately another ten percent, but it could be used as a wrapper, a carrier for the several large portions of boned meat. It's important to remember, though, that the individual portions should first be permitted to cool before being tightly wrapped for carrying. Even then, there is a risk that venison sealed off from the air will begin spoiling in transit. I once made the mistake of placing a cooled quarter of a venison carcass into a large plastic garbage bag for temporary storage. One of my hunting buddies was planning on stopping by that evening to get the quarter, but he was delayed until the next morning, and I, in the meantime, forgot about the plastic wrapper. When my buddy finally arrived, scarcely more than twelve hours after the quarter had been placed in the bag, he discovered that part of the meat was already tainted. We salvaged most of it by discarding some and treating the rest with a vinegar rinse. But I've never forgotten how rapidly that spoilage took place in the absence of circulating air. Similarly, if a deer carcass has to be left in the woods for a few hours, prop the gutted carcass partway off the ground so that a cooling air circulation can occur around all surfaces. Otherwise, the earth will insulate the downward side, keeping the warmth within the carcass.

Carrying by Vehicle

All right, now let's change the subject to a different kind of transporting. We are finally at the roadside (whew!), and now we can load the deer onto our vehicle. How great it will feel to rest our weary bones during the ride home. Oh yes, there's still some coffee left in the thermos! But first, let's secure the deer carcass on, or in, the vehicle. Many states require that a deer carcass, or a tagged portion of the carcass, be visible during transport on public highways. Yes, I understand the logic behind that kind of law, but I don't necessarily agree that the logic was good. A poacher is not going to purposely let a deer carcass be seen anyway. Regardless, we (the good guys) often have to carry our deer carcasses on the outside of the vehicle, and this can pose a real problem to sedan owners, considering the design of most modern cars. There's no place to tie the rope! And no longer are there any bubble fenders, arched tail fins, running boards, or any of those other classy design features that once were so useful to the deer hunter. With a station wagon or pickup truck, there's no problem; you just lay the deer in the back and leave the tailgate down, if necessary. The only space on a sedan suitable for transporting a deer is on the roof or the trunk. If the trunk is loaded with camping gear or whatever, the roof is obviously your only remaining option. So, you'd better have plenty of rope available to permit connections with all four ends of the front and rear bumpers. A fifty-foot roll of quarter-inch nylon cord might seem like more than you would need, but it's better to have too much than too little. If your journey home will require several hours of travel, and if the carcass has not yet had a chance to completely cool, then shims of some sort should be placed under the carcass so that heat cannot build up on the homeward ride. The shims can be improvised from tightly-rolled newspapers or any other non-scratching material that will permit air to circulate freely around all sides of the carcass without harming the car paint.

An even better way to transport a deer carcass outside a sedan is to use a removable cartop carrier. These usually are of adjustable length and can be stored in the trunk until needed. Most designs are made to hook onto the rain gutters above the door frames and so they will securely fit just about any make of car. The advantages of a cartop carrier are that their raised struts allow cooling air to pass underneath the carcass and that only a few yards of rope are necessary to batten down the load.

Again, if the journey is to be a long one, perhaps even with an overnight stay involved along the way, always keep the fact in mind that your topside cargo consists of highly perishable and highly valuable meat. At rest stops, park in the shade. If warm weather begins to threaten, consider placing bags of ice inside the deer. Don't take chances with the quality of your venison. That's *food* up there on the roof!

Chapter 5

Skinning and Care of Hides

Warm vs. Cold Skinning

There is more involved with skinning a deer than just the "how-to" aspect. We should also take a look at the "where-to" and the "when-to." After all, we need a place in which to work that might not necessarily be the same location where we plan to hang and age the venison and later butcher the carcass. Our buck might also be a potential trophy, in which case special treatment is required. If we know these situations in advance, they can have some bearing on whether we will skin the deer now or later. We're not looking at critical decisions here but are instead just considering all the possibilities.

But one fact is certain: the hide comes off a deer much more easily if the carcass is still warm. Not just a little more, but a *lot* more easily. Many hunters of my acquaintance skin their deer no later than the evening of the day of the kill, and some of them literally rush home so that the skinning chore can be done at earliest convenience.

The problem with cold skinning is that a layer of fat underneath the hide begins to harden into a tough, tallowlike substance as soon as the carcass cools below body temperature. The hide itself also becomes less flexible. Skinning a cold deer carcass can be a difficult chore, but certainly not an impossible one. In many instances, there is ample justification for leaving the hide on a deer until the time for butchering arrives.

For example, many hunters claim that the hide protects the carcass from excessive drying during the hanging and aging process. Maybe so. The thick layer of hair on a deer hide also serves to partially insulate the carcass against sudden changes in outdoor temperature; that is, the carcass will be slower to heat up during the day, and to freeze at night, if the natural blanket of the hide is left on a deer. A carcass should not be permitted to freeze for a number of reasons (see chapter 7 for at least a couple of good ones), but a carcass frozen with the skin still attached poses a very serious problem. In order to thaw a deer for skinning, you need both heat and the passage of time, and that combination can spoil the venison. The outer surfaces of the carcass will be thawed (and spoiling) long before the regions deeper in the meat are thawed. Certainly, if you have no other place to hang your deer than on a tree limb in the backyard, then you should leave the hide on until the deer can be skinned, quartered, and relocated to a more sheltered area.

But under most circumstances, it doesn't make one real whit of difference to the venison whether you leave the hide on for a while or take it off at the earliest opportunity. If the deer is to be mounted, however, early skinning helps insure that the hair will remain intact on the finished mount.

Skinning is probably the most cumbersome and space-demanding step in the rendering of a deer for consumption. Quartering, which can be done as soon as the skinning is done, also is most easily performed on a hanging carcass. However, once these two steps are completed, the subsequent steps of meat aging and final butchering can be accomplished elsewhere. I make this point because many successful hunters do not have a barn, a garage, or other unheated structure in which an entire deer can be conveniently hung intact for prolonged aging and subsequent butchering. Actually, once the carcass has been skinned and quartered, even city apartment dwellers can enjoy the full benefits of the final steps of do-it-yourself venison butchering. The major portions of a quartered deer can even be fitted into a refrigerator for temporary storage. This may pose a problem with where to keep the milk and eggs, but that's what neighbors are for. (Use those good people; they were probably expecting a couple of free venison steaks anyway.)

Work Space Requirements

An unheated attic, enclosed back porch, a cool basement, and other such areas can be utilized for the clean and protected storage of skinned venison quarters. Even prolonged meat aging can be achieved if these areas are continually cool, which usually depends on the weather. The only real problem for many folks is a lack of a place in which the deer can initially be skinned and quartered. Knowing that such a work space need only be a temporary set-up, certain improvisations can be made on that basis. Actually, it is possible to take those improvisations a little too far.

Ground Skinning — Not Recommended

I once stuck myself with the job of skinning a deer on the ground. Yes, it is possible to do it that way. I was fortunate in that a heavy snowfall had occurred, and I subsequently didn't have to worry about getting the venison dirty. While muttering various oaths regarding the lack of trees in the vicinity, I tackled the job head on and was soon deeply involved in what must have appeared to be a form of Eskimo mud wrestling. The main problem was that I had no resistance to tug against. I'd pull the skin, and the deer would slide towards me. I traveled more miles pulling that deer around in little circles than I had in stalking this same critter. By the time I was finished, the packed snow in the area revealed many footsteps, the wide grooves of a deer carcass in hot pursuit of those footsteps, and several outlines of my body where I had fallen down.

This is not a recommended method for skinning a deer. But, with certain improvements, ground skinning is a viable option if there is simply no way in which the deer can be hung upright for skinning. In the absence of snow cover, a sheet of polyethylene plastic sheeting could be substituted to protect the exposed venison. Another improvement would be to get an assistant skinner ("But honey, I had other plans!"), and failing that, to at least be able to tie one end of the deer to an anchor of some sort. Once this latter item is accom-

plished, the deer could conceivably even be skinned with the help
of an automobile, as explained later in this chapter under the "power
steering method."

Two Basic Techniques

Although there are several different ways to approach the chore
of skinning a deer, there are really only two basic techniques by which
the skin comes off intact. In the most common technique, the skin
comes off as a square rug, released from the carcass via cuts along
the inseams of all four legs and the belly cut, which was done earlier
when the deer was gutted. The other technique is used when a deer
is to be mounted as a trophy, and considerably different methods
are needed.

But, let me say right here that the person most qualified for the
trophy skinning is the taxidermist. Many hunters don't realize that
their taxidermists would actually prefer to do the caping and, consequently, these hunters often burden themselves with a stint of
demanding work that could be better performed in a few easy minutes
by a professional. I'm referring here to the complete job of caping
that includes skinning around the antlers, eyes, ears, and nose, with
follow-up steps that include sawing off the skull cap and the removing of cartilage from within the ears. In most cases, unless you are
either doing your own amateur taxidermy, or have been hunting in
such a remote region that you can't get to a taxidermist's shop within
several days, then your best bet is to arrange for a professional to
do the full caping. The complete details of caping are explained in
chapter 13 under do-it-yourself taxidermy. There is a simpler method
of caping, which I will now describe, that saves you from having
to haul the entire deer to the taxidermist's shop, yet which leaves
the bulk of the detailed skinning in the hands of the professional.

Rough Caping

Rough caping consists of removing the head with the neck skin
still intact. Start with a cut that encircles the deer from the top of
the shoulders to down around the chest just in front of the legs. You
want to provide the taxidermist with more skin than he (or she) will
actually need for the typical shoulder mount. Surplus hide can later

be cut away when the deer is mounted on a plaque, but a shortage of hide can never be replaced satisfactorily. Peel the skin down until the base of the skull is reached. Then, either saw through the neck to free the head, or cut through the flesh with a knife, and twist the head to break the spine. No other cuts are made. You are left with a deer head to which is attached a cylinder of neck hide. This can be stored in the refrigerator or other cool place until the trip to the taxidermist can be made. But don't wait too long. The first thing that any taxidermist does when he is presented with a deer head for mounting is grasp some of the hairs between his fingers and try to pluck them out. If a tuft of hair pulls free, you have delayed too long and the deer should not be mounted. If the head is kept in a refrigerator, you can probably get away with a two- or three-day delay, but don't push your luck. I'm telling you this before I go on to describe another alternative, one for storing a deer head until it can be mounted. This second method involves freezing the potential trophy, wrapped in a plastic garbage bag to retard freezer burn. Freezing permits you to take a little extra time to decide whether the deer really deserves trophy status. You might decide, once the thrill of accomplishment has worn thin, that just an antler mount, rather than a full shoulder mount, is what you really want or can afford. On the other hand, if the passage of time does not diminish the trophy value or the importance of having it mounted, then you can proceed to the taxidermist with full confidence in your actions. There is a small risk, however, that the hide and hair can be damaged by freezing, sometimes to the extent that the trophy becomes worthless for mounting. Because the antlers take up such a large space within the plastic bag, there is often sufficient air present for the freezer burn to begin, which can dehydrate the skin and weaken the hair follicles. Some of that air can be removed by sucking it out via a straw inserted through the bag opening, but not all of it. Another way around this is to poke the antlers through the side of the bag and then tape the holes shut around the base of the antlers. Another possible problem occurs when the head is to be thawed — that old bugaboo combination of time and temperature which can cause a spoilage during thawing. Remove the plastic while the deer head is thawing so that air can reach the hide to help keep it dry and to slow the renewed growth of bacteria. Call the taxidermist in advance and describe your situation; he might want you to keep the

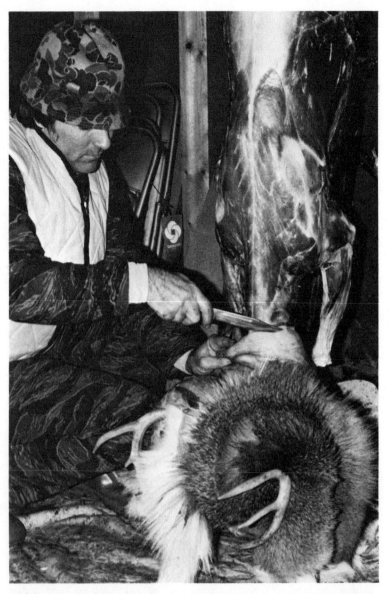

Fig. 16. "Rough caping" is done if the head is to be transported to a taxidermist for mounting. With the deer hung head-down, peel the hide down to the base of the skull and then sever the neck.

head frozen until he can work on it, or he may have a freezer right there in the shop.

The rough caping method can be performed on the carcass while it is laying on the ground, or it can be done more easily with a carcass that has been suspended from its hind legs. If the carcass is suspended in this manner, with the head positioned downward, you really don't have to make the cut encircling the shoulders. You can instead just leave the entire hide attached to the head after both have been removed from the carcass. Surprisingly, nearly a third of the hide is used in a full shoulder mount, and the hide that remains is usually too small to be used in making garments other than gloves and similar small items.

Whether to Skin Head-Up or Head-Down

There is a surprisingly high degree of biased and opinionated thinking among those of us who do our own deer processing. Some of us believe that venison should be butchered fresh; others swear that venison is not palpatable until it has been aged for weeks. On the subject of cooking venison, we argue over the merits of "rare" versus "well done". There is even considerable controversy between hunters as to whether a deer should be hung head-up or head-down for skinning. More than a few hunters have adamantly told me that hanging a deer with the head up is absolutely the wrong way to do it. When I press for explanations, though, I never get any satisfactory answers. Personal preferences, it sometimes seems, can be as rigid as a brick wall. The fact of the matter, however, is that the "best" way is the one that is best adapted to a particular situation. The venison from a tough old buck should be aged, but portions of a sweet young doe can be eaten at the earliest possible time. Certain cuts of venison from a deer can be served well cooked, and other cuts from the same deer will be somewhat more tender if served pink-in-the-middle. As for hanging a deer for skinning, the best way will depend upon what you plan to do with the deer.

A deer that is to be caped for taxidermy work should be hung with the head down because this position provides better access to the head and gives you the advantage of greater leverage for peeling off the hide from around the neck. On the other hand, if the deer

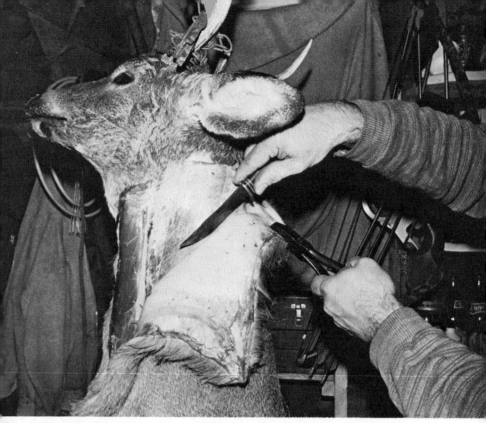

Fig. 17. *Step 1*—If the deer will not be mounted, begin skinning with an incision around the neck. Extend the belly cut up to the chin. Use pliers to help pull the skin free of the neck area.

is instead hung by the antlers, only a single rope is needed, and the carcass can more conveniently be quartered and partially butchered using the boneless butchering techniques described in chapter 6. The head-up position is also required for the "power-steering" method, which is described later. So, hang the deer in whichever position is best for your particular situation; head-down for caping, head-up for easier quartering. The skin comes off either way.

Where to Hang

To hang a deer for skinning, a bare minimum of seven feet of height is required, although more is better. The average adult whitetail deer can stand on hind legs to pluck an apple from that high off the ground. Many an overhanging tree branch has served as a temporary meat pole. So have saplings, tied to form tripods. Even trees having no lower branches can be used to hang a deer by cinching a rope high around the trunk and using that as the support. Gate posts, children's swing sets, clothesline poles, porch swing hooks, propped ladders, and a host of other contrivances have been temporarily commandeered for deer-hanging duties. All these are outdoor arrangements, and that's fine when the weather cooperates, but indoor skinning and quartering in an unheated structure is the way to go if you can swing it. If there are no beams or joists over which a rope can be thrown, install a size "O" ceiling hook, or two hooks a yard apart if the deer is to be hung head down. Make sure your attachments are sturdy because they're going to be asked to withstand considerable tugging during skinning. Hemp rope, rather

Fig. 18. *Step 2*—Grasp the loosened hide with both hands and peel it down to the shoulders.

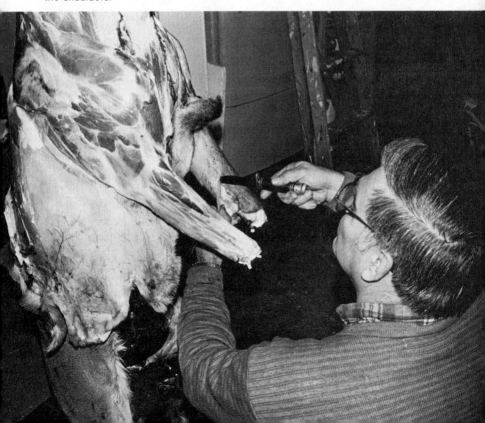

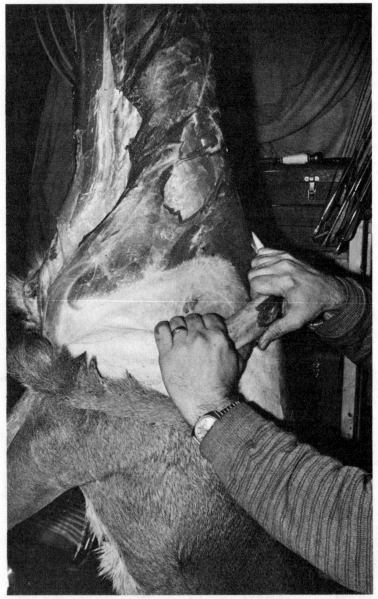

Fig. 19. *Step 3*—Remove the lower portions of the front legs by sawing or by cutting the tendons with a knife. Then slit the "inseam" of each leg.

than nylon, is best for hanging deer because it doesn't stretch and cause the carcass to bounce while you're struggling with skinning.

Head-Up Skinning

Use head-up hanging if the deer is not going to be mounted as a trophy. In this position, the carcass can more easily be quartered one section at a time without your having to rearrange the placement of the deer.

For a buck having spreading antlers, loop the rope around the base of both antlers and tie securely. With a doe or a spike buck, however, the rope must be fastened around the neck, just below the jaw, with the knot located at the rear of the head. Either a slip knot or a square knot will serve the purpose.

Now you're ready to remove the lower portions of all four legs. This can be done either with a bone saw or ordinary carpenter's crosscut saw, or you can simply cut into the first joint of each leg with a knife to sever the ligaments. It is important that the legs not be cut any shorter than those first joints because you might later want to hang the individual quartered sections for aging. By making a slit under the main tendon where it connects with the severed joint, you create a convenient opening so that the quarter can be hung on a nail.

The actual skinning begins now. If you have not already done so, extend the cut from the gutted belly and chest all the way up the front of the throat to the base of the jaw. Easy: don't cut the rope too! Then cut the hide all the way around the neck parallel to the encircling rope. I perform this otherwise awkward incision by "walking" the knife. First, I probe the tip of the knife in about an inch under the skin, and then I pull the knife handle outward, as though the knife were a lever, so that the blade edge cuts the skin from underneath.

The "walking" method greatly reduces hair fallout. That's a real bonus because wherever loose deer hair comes in contact with the bare carcass, there it sticks. Deer hair not only is unsightly on the dinner platter, but it also tends to impart a musky odor to the venison. These loose hairs can later be removed from the carcass by wiping with a vinegar-soaked cloth, but your best bet is to try to avoid the hair fallout in the first place.

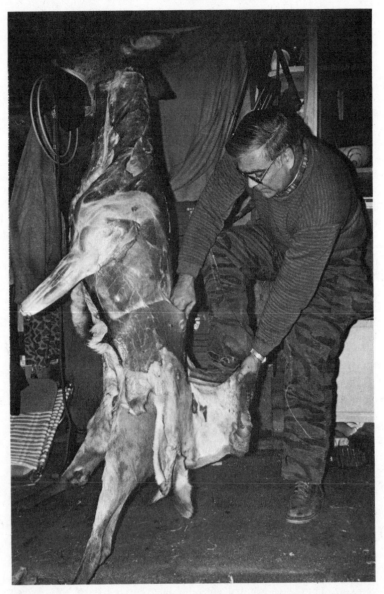

Fig. 20. *Step 4*—After working the hide off the front legs, continue peeling downwards. Skip Sheesley here demonstrates some fancy footwork for speeding up skinning.

The hide must now be peeled back from the neck. A pair of pliers will speed up this process. Grasp the edge of the hide and pull, using the knife only when the underlying red meat shows signs of adhering to the hide. Work the hide down the neck until it can finally be temporarily draped over the deer's back.

Before proceeding any further, turn your attention to the two front legs. Make a slit along the inseam of each leg until the central chest and belly cut is reached. Use the knife "walking" method described a few moments ago. Start at the outer end of each leg and walk the knife towards the chest. These two cuts (one for each leg) make it possible to peel the neck hide down over and below the shoulders. Getting over the hump of the shoulders is the most difficult step in deer skinning because there is almost always a very thick layer of tallow under the skin at this point. Sometimes it is difficult to even see where the tallow ends and the skin begins. Use the skinning knife liberally, but be careful that you don't nick the underside of the hide.

Finally, the shoulders will give way, and the skinning chore will be easy sledding from here on out. The stretch from shoulders to hips is comparatively easy, and you might not need to use the knife at all. Using both hands, grasp the flesh side of the hide where it curls away from the carcass and pull downward. In tough spots, strike downward on this curl with your fist.

When you get as far as the deer's hips, the final stage of skinning can be speeded up by putting your weight into the job. Grab hold of the outer edge of the loose hide and place your foot up on the flap of hide. Push your foot down while continuing to hold the hide. When the butt of the tailbone is exposed, cut this appendage off so that the tailbones remain with the skin. Finally, you can peel the hide down off the hind legs as though it were a pair of thermal underwear. Or, if you prefer, cut the inseams of the hind legs before making that last pull over the hips. I prefer to cut the inseams in the hide after it has been completely removed because the bare carcass is that much less apt to come in contact with loose hairs.

Head-Down Skinning

Use head-down skinning if the deer is to be caped for mounting because this position provides you with more convenient access to

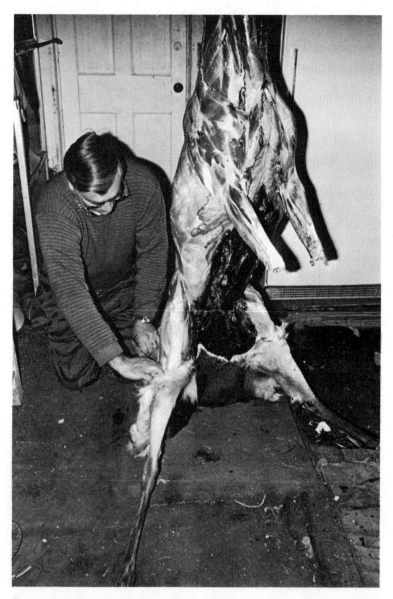

Fig. 21. *Step 5*—Leaving the hind legs in contact with the floor prevents the carcass from swinging. Don't remove them until after skinning is finished. It is not necessary to slit the hind leg "inseams" of the hide until it is off the deer.

the head and neck. Also, you can get better leverage for caping if the deer is hung head-down. However, head-down skinning is slightly more complicated in the early stages and creates need for a little extra work when the quartering is done.

Remove the lower portions of both hind legs using the sawing or cutting methods used in the prior head-up skinning section. You might also want to do the front legs at this point in time, but it's easier if you postpone doing so until the deer has been hung in position. While the deer carcass is still lying on the ground, slit the hide up the inseams of both hind legs until the crotch is reached. Do that by slipping the knife blade under the skin so that you cut by pulling the knife outward. This reduces the amount of hair that would otherwise be loosened by the knife. Then peel the hide away from the severed joints (where the lower legs were removed) to expose the large tendons which connect at this point. These connections will provide you with convenient handles from which the deer can be hung. There are now two methods by which the carcass can be supported upright. Either insert a sturdy four-foot pole behind the tendons of both legs and use this pole as the hanger, or else use rope to tie each leg to a ceiling hook. These hooks should be spaced about thirty-six inches apart so the legs will be spread for easier skinning. Lifting the deer into position for hanging is an awkward and difficult chore unless you have either a block-and-tackle or a willing assistant.

Now that the deer is hung in position, peel the hide down each hind leg. Then cut the tailbone when it begins to show. The hide will come off the hips fairly easily, although you might have to make a knife cut here and there to free the hide from adhering fat or muscle. Similarly, the waist and chest regions will not offer much resistance. Pulling the skin downward is usually the only effort that is really necessary. If you are wondering when we are going to begin caping, read on, we're almost there. If the front lower legs have not yet been removed, and if the inseams have not already been slit to the chest, then do this now.

Proceed with the skinning until the hide has been pulled *halfway* over the shoulders. Then, if caping is to be done, stop! Now the first step of caping can be performed by cutting the hide from inside out, rather than from outside in. This results in considerably less damage to the hair and lets you make a more even and sym-

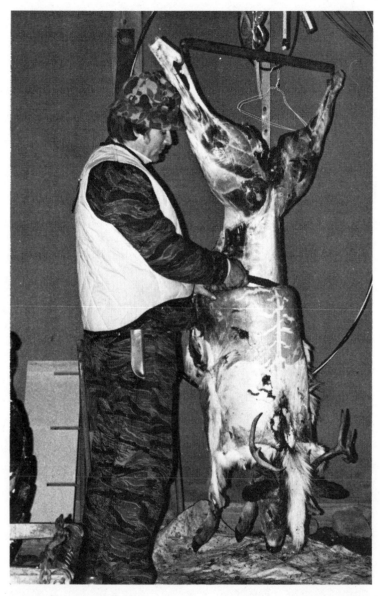

Fig. 22. The head-down skinning method, as illustrated here, should be used if the deer is to be caped for mounting. This position provides easy access to the head and neck.

metrical cut all the way around the carcass. After you've done this, the hide from the lower body (the hips and waist) will fall free of the carcass. Another advantage of delaying caping until the upper body has been skinned is that, because you make the inside out cut with the hide somewhat removed from the body of the deer, a second starting step with pliers is not required. You can instead just grasp the remaining flap of the hide and continue pulling it down over the neck until the base of the skull is reached. Now the neck can be severed, either by sawing or by cutting and twisting, to release the head from the body. This is rough caping. A long cylindrical cape of neck hide will remain attached to the head, and you can transport this trophy portion of the deer, as is, to the taxidermist.

If you plan to do your own taxidermy, or otherwise have reason to perform a fully professional caping, see chapter 13 for the details on the extra, finishing steps of caping and skull preparation that are necessary for do-it-yourself taxidermy.

The Alternate Power-Steering Method

This is a third technique for skinning a deer, and it requires the least physical effort. The power-steering method consists of using the power of an automobile (or a placid horse) to do the work of pulling and tugging. A job that can ordinarily require a half hour or more can be done in just a few minutes. The drawbacks to this method are that you need just the right setup to be able to accomplish the feat, and the fact that the hide or even the carcass can be damaged if special care is not taken to prevent it.

Hang the deer in the head-up position and make sure that the rope and the support are sufficiently sturdy for the task ahead. Just as was done in the head-up skinning procedure described earlier, remove all four lower legs, slit the inseams, and slit up the full length of the throat to the jaw. Extend a cut around the neck just below the head and pull the hide about a foot down the back of the neck. This will provide a flap of hide to which the towing rope can be attached. Because the towing rope would be apt to slip free of the hide under the force of pulling if it were merely tied to the hide, a special trick is needed. Insert a rock about the size of a golf ball (or what the heck, use a real golf ball) under the skin so that a bulge is formed large enough that the towing rope can be tied around it.

Back the vehicle into place, tie the other end of the tow rope to the bumper, put 'er in gear and *slowly* drive a few inches away from the hanging deer. Forget all those daydreams about being able to brag to folks how you skinned a deer in five seconds flat. Get out of the car to make sure that you've got things lined up correctly and that there is no venison adhering to the skin. Excessive enthusiasm can cost you many pounds of valuable venison and a ruined hide. Drive ahead another few inches, check the deer again, and continue this slow progress until you have either skinned the deer or (1) have pulled a tree out by the roots, or (2) a garage off its foundation. Beware the forces loosed by Detroit and others. A task that used to be achieved by the power of a single horse requires somewhat more self control and caution when it is performed with the power of hundreds of horses.

The Value of Deerhide

Although I have skinned many deer, I am always surprised anew by the luxuriant heaviness of the pelt and by the contradictory smallness of that natural garment when it has been removed from the carcass. Even though I may plan to sell a particular deerhide, I still feel a temporary possessiveness towards it. Animal hides have been used by humankind for many thousands, perhaps even millions, of years, and yet, even though we now have access to a wide variety of exotic space-age fabrics, natural leathers are still superior in many regards. Leather has the ability to "sweat," to release body heat, is scuff resistant, and performs well at sub-zero temperatures where synthetic substitutes crack and fail. A deerhide is a valuable piece of property. Of course, if you sell it as a raw skin, the value received will be at its lowest point. Depending upon the prevailing hide market prices, you might get enough through the sale of a deerhide to cover, say, your hunting license fee. That's something, but it's not a lot. However, if you tan the hide and do nothing more than that to it, the hide increases in value by more than five times the raw value. If you convert this natural deer garment into gloves, steering wheel covers, moccasins, belts, handbags, wallets, vests, holsters, or a host of other items, the value of a deerskin skyrockets. A hard decision awaits you when a deer has been skinned. To sell "as is" or not to

Fig. 23. A fur buyer/taxidermist examines the quality of a raw deerskin.

sell, that is the proverbial question. You want my advice? Keep it, tan it, use it. Seldom will you get a similar opportunity to convert a few hours of leisure time into such a profitable venture. You might reap that profit only in the form of personal possession, but does that decrease the value? No, it sure doesn't!

Salting and Care of Hides

Once a deer has been skinned, the hide should be given, at the very least, sufficient attention to insure that it won't spoil. All the value of a deer carcass does not rest solely in the venison; to throw the hide away would be a terrible waste of a truly natural resource. If the weather is cool, I usually wait half a day or so before picking off the clumps of fat and flesh that usually remain adhered to the bare side of the hide. By draping the freshly skinned hide temporarily over a pole or railing, enough air drying takes place in that short a time that the hide can then be cleaned more easily and neatly. A freshly skinned hide is slippery on the underside and subsequently is difficult to scrape and clean. A slightly dried skin better reveals the existence of adhesions and lets you remove them more easily. A sharp knife is *not* necessary. A butter knife is adequate and helps you avoid nicks.

If the skin is to be sold, only a superficial cleaning of the bare side is required, and even then only because a fatty, uncleaned hide is apt to begin spoiling before it can be transported to the buyer. Any deerhide will be judged by the buyer more on the basis of the hide's ability to resist a tug of the hair than by any other criteria. Loose hair indicates that spoilage has already begun, even though the hide may not yet have developed a rank odor. Bullet holes can detract somewhat from the value if there is an excessive number of them in the prime regions of the hide. And, of course, a small hide from a yearling won't bring as many dollars as a larger hide from a monster buck. Spoilage, however, leaves no room for bargaining; a hide is either unspoiled or it is worthless. There is no in-between. If the hide can be transported to the buyer (usually a taxidermist, or perhaps a fur dealer) within a couple of days, no extra care of the hide is required; that is, you can delay for a short time if the weather remains cold or if the hide can somehow be stuffed into the refrigerator. But even then, you're taking a chance on ruining

Fig. 24. *Step 1*—A hide can be temporarily preserved with either uniodized salt or borax. Rub briskly into the flesh side surface.

a perfectly good hide. The best bet is to salt the hide as soon as the adhering fat has been removed.

Use common uniodized salt or dairy salt. Rock salt is too coarse, and table salt, which contains iodine, should not be used because iodine can have an adverse effect on the appearance of a tanned hide. Another substance which works well is borax. A suitable form of borax can be purchased in most supermarkets as "Boraxo," a laundry powder. Both salt and borax preserve hides effectively for temporary storage by drawing the moisture from the skin and by creating an environment that is hostile to the growth of bacteria. About five pounds of either salt or borax is sufficient for salting a hide. Ideally, the hide will be salted at least twice.

For the first salting, firmly rub the salt or borax onto every square inch of the bare side of the hide. Then, fold the hide over to sand-

Fig. 25. *Step 2—*Fold salted hide over, flesh side in, and roll up into a bundle.

wich the bare side against itself. Roll the hide up like a rug and store it overnight in a cool, dry place. The next day, unroll the hide to remove the old salt. You will discover that much of the salt will have dissolved or is otherwise very crumbly and sticky. Scrape all this old salt off the hide and discard it.

Now that much of the moisture has been removed from the hide, a second coating of salt or borax can be applied. You might consider repeating the first step again to remove more moisture, and that would be a good idea because there's no such thing as too much salting when it comes to caring for a hide. If the hide is to be sold, then roll it up again and tuck it back in cold storage. A hide that is permitted to dry outstretched will become stiffer than a sheet of wallboard, and trying to cram one of these full-width hides into a Volkswagen is an event to remember.

Many people who tan deerhides claim that a better job of tanning can be done, and in less time, if the hide is first salted. That makes good sense because, if the original moistures have been drawn out of a hide by salting, the slightly porous membrane of the hide will more easily be able to soak up the tanning chemicals.

Hides can be wrapped in plastic and frozen for long term storage once they have been properly salted. However, a rolled-up hide, with all that long, thick hair, will require nearly as much freezer space as will the boned venison from the entire deer carcass.

Chapter 6

Venison and How to Butcher It

Nutritional Value of Venison

Venison, when properly prepared, is a culinary delight that holds its own in the company of fine wines and other condiments. The meat has a fine-grained, interesting texture, yet is tender without being mushy as are some of the more expensive cuts of domestic meats. But the good news doesn't end here. Not only is venison delicious, it also is better for your nutritional well-being than are most commercially available meats. In this day and age when so many tasty items have been found to be either worthless or even potentially harmful to your health, rest assured that venison compares favorably with the supermarket alternatives. Venison is low in fat and calories and is high in minerals and vitamins. It also is free from chemical additives and other nasty substances.

Some of venison's nutritional superiority exists solely by the default of our modern meat raising systems. However, the basic fact remains that whitetail deer are highly efficient processors of the natural foods they eat. The buds, herbs, acorns, wild fruits, and other browse in a deer's diet are effectively converted into muscle, and the benefits of this natural food fare are passed along to those of us who enjoy venison.

The following chart shows the nutritional values of venison in comparison to several different cuts and types of domestic meats. This nutritional chart should not be interpreted to mean that all cuts of all domestic meat are inferior to venison. However, when compared against the popular cuts of beef, pork, lamb, and fowl, it soon becomes obvious that venison ranks very high by modern dietary standards. For one thing, the fat content, and consequently the caloric count, are extremely low. Even when all excess fat has been trimmed from a beefsteak or other commercial cut, there still remains a high level of fatty tissue entwined within the muscle fibers of domestic red meat. When a portion of venison is trimmed of fat, the remaining meat is 97.8 percent fat-free. Now that's what you can properly call lean meat! Pound for pound, venison has an average of less than half the calories found in well-marbled, fatty cuts of beef, pork and lamb.

Venison also contains comparably high levels of calcium, magnesium, phosphorous, and iron. These minerals are essential to our well-being, and it's great that we can partake of them while enjoying a gourmet venison meal. And let's not forget the vitamins; venison scores high in thiamine, riboflavin, and niacin. In fact, it has been calculated that a one-pound venison steak contains more than the full recommended daily adult allowances for thiamine and niacin and a major share of the recommended riboflavin allowance. These are *natural* vitamins, products of nature rather than of industry, and they come to you indirectly in venison from the foods of the forest.

Gourmet Food on a Survivor's Budget

Good food is somewhat expensive, sure, but the cost of true gourmet food is out of sight. Even to enjoy the experience of grilling an ordinary beefsteak in the backyard, the average person has to scrimp elsewhere to be able to partake of this luxury. We would like to be able to experiment with different sauces and exotic recipes, but with meat prices so high we restrict our culinary adventures to within the affordable and commonplace. We instead apply our skills to the preparation of tossed salads and hamburger. Why take a chance with big money, right?

NUTRITIONAL VALUES OF VENISON AND CERTAIN CUTS OF DOMESTIC MEATS
(Cooked Portions of 3½ oz.)

Meat	Proximate (g.)			Minerals (mg.)				Vitamins (mg.)		
	Calories	Protein	Fat	Calcium	Magnesium	Phosphorous	Iron	Thiamine	Riboflavin	Niacin
Venison	146	29.5	2.2	20	29	264	3.5	0.37	0.28	7.4
Beef Porterhouse (lean and marbled)	242	25.4	14.7	11	20	183	3.8	0.10	0.12	6.1
Ground Beef Sirloin	408	22.2	34.7	10	21	186	2.9	0.06	0.18	4.6
Pork Loin Chop (lean and fat)	357	29.4	25.6	12	22	229	4.4	1.18	0.19	5.5
Fresh Ham (lean, marbled and fat)	306	32.9	18.3	6	26	263	2.3	0.57	0.27	4.5
Lamb Loin Chop	302	23.0	22.5	10	20	193	3.0	0.17	0.27	6.5
Chicken Broiler	136	23.8	3.8	9	–	201	1.7	0.05	0.19	8.8
Domestic Turkey (white meat)	176	32.9	3.9	5	28	185	1.2	0.14	0.03	–

Compiled from "Food Values of Portions Commonly Used" by Pennington and Church (Harper & Row, 1980)

Well, with a supply of venison stocked away in the freezer, we can experiment to our heart's content. Make no mistake about it, venison qualifies as a gourmet delicacy in every sense of the word. Venison has a distinctive flavor, responds well to special cooking techniques, is uniquely different from domestic meats, and last but not least, is difficult to obtain. Venison also enjoys the status of being exclusive because wild venison cannot be legally sold or purchased. (The venison occasionally shown on some menus often originates from the red deer of Scotland.) Restaurants charge exorbitant prices for such exotics as truffles, caviar, morels, lobster, escargots, and other choice items that are obtained chiefly not from domestic sources but from the natural world. Truffles, for example, are unique little black mushrooms that grow out of sight, just under the surface of French soil. Trained pigs are sometimes used to locate truffles for their handlers, who then dig up these delicious morsels and ship them off to market. When you finally are served truffles in a fine restaurant, the cost will be high. (Trained pigs are hard to find.)

But then, so would venison be expensive; that is, if you could buy it. If you had to pick up the tab for someone else's hunting trip every time you had a venison meal, you would soon come to understand the real meaning of the words "exclusive" and "expensive." The fact that we hunt for pleasure, rather than for food or profit, does not alter the fact that venison has all the qualifications of a gourmet food. The fact that venison during the Depression gained the name of "government beef" also does not change the status of venison. Fine cuisine is what it is. If we treat a flavorful meat the way a connoiseur would, then we will not be misled into thinking that just because a certain food is temporarily plentiful, it is also commonplace. Unfortunately (or perhaps fortunately), there are those among us who claim that venison or any wild game has a wild taste that makes it unpalatable. Well, as long as "wild" means somehow different rather than spoiled (which is sometimes the case if we aren't careful), they can be right.

Yes, there is a difference between venison and domestic meats, and it depends only on your perspective whether this is a good or a bad difference. There is also a difference as to whether you look at venison as being a gourmet food or a less than adequate beef substitute. A lot has been written about how venison can be made to taste just like beef so that those people who profess not to like wild game would not be able to tell the difference. That certainly is true; with a little cover-up here and there, venison can be made to pass for beef. But why would you want to do a thing like that? Why try to alter a gourmet food into being something ordinary?

Venison should be appreciated for its own merits, much the same way that you relish a lobster for its sweet, succulent flavor. Sure, you could prepare lobster in ways that would disguise the ocean smell, and you could probably get rid of that wild flavor, but that would also destroy your appreciation of lobster.

Similarly, venison should not automatically be dummied up with strongly flavored sauces solely to change the taste of it into something that could be mistaken for a domestic meat. Take the approach of the gourmet and limit the use of sauces to only those which will enhance the natural taste and flavor of venison. A fine wine, good music in the background, candles (optional), the children either young and in bed, or grown and off someplace (also optional), and a fine meal of venison with the proper accompaniments — what else could you possibly ask in the way of a gourmet meal of fine cuisine?

The Tragedy of Modern Domestic Meats

Sometimes you can get as many chuckles from reading the advertising hype on a package of processed supermarket meat as you can from the comic section of the weekend newspapers. Seems that meat is inevitably packaged under brand names that are designed to evoke images of sunshine, shade trees, sparkling brooks and so on, scenes where children soar kites under perpetually blue skies and Mom is in the kitchen forever baking apple pies. This advertising often contains a picture, typically one that shows a smiling, straw-hatted farmer feeding only two or three head of livestock. Even the livestock are smiling (although somewhat ironically). You get the mental picture, standing there in the supermarket, that the contents of the package you are holding were grown back in the Good Old Days and then were mysteriously transported into the Here and Now, just for you. You even feel strangely reassured that those little piggies (or whatever) in the picture received many affectionate pats on the rump during their rich and full lives down on the farm.

It's good if you can enjoy such scenario at the supermarket because you are paying through the nose for it and deserve to at least get some entertainment for your money—something, that is, besides a flavorless blend of hydrocarbons called "meat." This is not to say that small scale livestock raising is no longer in existence. No, there are still many small-time and part-time farming operations in America where smiling people carefully nurture a few head of livestock. However, can you guess why these people are smiling? It's because they are planning to keep that meat for themselves! Home-raised meats are tastier, better grained and better textured. When you've got it, you keep it.

Modern meat growing operations are huge affairs, often involving a large staff of employees who, directly and indirectly, help care for herds of livestock that might number well into the thousands. These livestock have been genetically and chemically engineered to grow as large as possible in as short a time as possible. Time is money, especially when it is spent just ambling around on four legs eating expensive grains and food supplements. Actually, sometimes the feed isn't all that great. Often, before beef cattle are completely switched over to a rich diet of fattening corn (which will make them sick if the switch is made too rapidly), a portion of sawdust or chopped corncobs is added to the diet. This prevents the stomach from shrinking prior to that final fast-and-furious weight gain. In an industry where a week's delay can mean the difference between profit and loss, there simply isn't much time for smiles and pats on the rump.

What does all this have to do with whitetail deer? Well, the answer is in the fat and in the flavor. (Flavor? What's that?) Although we are truly fortunate that the livestock growers and processors have been able to adapt to rising production costs and still supply the demands of meat-hungry consumers, we have lost something along the way. We lost meat flavor, or most of it, and now have forgotten how it used to taste. Some people accuse venison of having a "wild" taste, a "gamey" flavor. My gosh! At least venison *tastes* like something. Unlike their domestic peers, deer eat a richly varied diet. Weight gain comes slowly, seldom if ever exceeding the need for a well developed musculature. Deer get plenty of exercise; they can easily jump the same fence that a fatted steer would have physical difficulty itching itself on a post thereof. Higher weight means more fat, and as long as we continue to pay for meat by-the-pound, commercial meats will be high in fat content. There's also the matter of age and maturity. Domestic meat animals grow large, due to infusions of growth hormones, but they seldom get a chance to grow up. For the sake of economic efficiency, cattle, pigs and sheep take the short walk down a long hall before their growth rates begin to level off. Thus, another reason exists for the lack of mature "character" and flavor in domestic meats. Yes, the meat is tender, but so is foam rubber.

On the average, deer advance to greater age and physical development. Although a substantial share of the total deer killed each year are only 1½ year-old spike and fork horn bucks—and that is not considered mature—the remaining 50-80 percent are 2½ years of age or more.

A varied diet, slow growth rate, exercise and maturity—these are the factors in an equation that adds up to genuine meat flavor. The next time you hear someone claim that venison has too strong a taste, tell them to go chew on a corncob. Venison definitely does, in fact, have a stronger flavor. The only question is, stronger than *what*?

Like We Said, a Truly "Lean" Meat

All the tallow (fat) and bone should be trimmed from venison before it is preserved or cooked in order to avoid the waxy taste that is otherwise produced. The tallow has a higher melting point than beef suet, and consequently it also solidifies faster when cooked venison begins to cool, forming little waxlike buttons that are not particularly palatable. Bone marrow also contains tallow, which oozes out during cooking if bones are left in a cut of meat. Like lamb, venison does not survive a long period of freezing unless the tallow and bone have been removed. Good flavor will otherwise be quickly lost.

After venison has been trimmed right down to the pure and tasty lean meat, it might appear that a deer carcass doesn't yield much meat at all. But, hold on there a minute! Just stop to consider how much fat and bone is usually included with most beefsteaks. In many of the more popular cuts of beefsteak, upwards of a third or more of the weight is taken up by fat and bone. You pay dearly for that extra weight too. There are at least three reasons why beefsteaks so often contain so much extra fat and bone. First, suet (beef fat), is the major source of the flavor in modern beef. In this day and age, a beefsteak that is not well-marbled and edged with fat will taste

Fig. 26. A typical beefsteak (left) and a venison steak (right). The "big package" beefsteak contains more fat and bone and less protein, iron, and vitamins.

rather bland (if it tastes like anything at all). Another reason is that the additional time and effort that would be required to trim beef down to lean meat would even further increase the cost at the check-out counter. The third reason is the "big package" hype. When you pay big money for a steak, you want to get something bigger than what can be totally hidden under a slice of bread. A steak that costs nearly as much as half a tank of gas had better be big or we would think twice about buying it. ("Oh no! The customer is thinking *twice!*")

Back to venison now. A venison steak, if properly trimmed, will cover a much smaller area on a dinner plate and yet provide just as much lean meat as a considerably larger beefsteak. This size difference should be remembered when divvying up a butchered carcass into serving size portions. Think small, not big. Try to picture how a slice of venison steak would appear if it were tucked up alongside a "T" bone and with a wide edging and tailing of suet wrapped around it. Then you can proceed with confidence that those little venison steaks will truly provide big meals.

Venison Butchering — Not That Big a Job

Whitetail deer truly deserve the title of "big game." When you see them standing long-legged in a field at twilight, their ears flared wide like hawk's wings, deer appear to be as large as domestic cattle. A buck, when flushed from his bed deep in the forest, bounds off into the shadows with all the explosive energy of a Brahma bull erupting from a chute at a rodeo. But let's not let these comparisons carry us too far away from reality. Certainly, whitetail deer are big game, but are they big? No, not really; deer are majestic, regal, and definitely one of the supreme trophies of North American wild game, but they actually are rather small.

A whitetail deer can slip right under the lowest strand of a barbed wire fence without hardly even slowing down from a full-speed gallop. It requires many complex physical attributes to achieve this feat, and being big isn't one of them. A standing deer's chest is less than eighteen to twenty inches off the ground. That's approximately the distance between your elbow and the tips of your fingers, and it helps explain why a wintering deer herd can have such a rough time after a heavy snowfall. An adult deer, field dressed, usually weighs less than 150 pounds, and more often than not, less than 130 pounds. Approximately half that weight is taken up by the hide, with its thick covering of hair, and the skeletal structure. The end result of the boneless butchering technique described in this chapter will be about one and a half cubic feet of venison. That's all. Of course, it will be all good lean meat, with no bones or fat to take up unnecessary space in your freezer, but there is nevertheless not a great deal of meat on a deer.

I'm not trying to belittle the value of the whitetail deer as a source of edible protein, but I do want to make the point that venison butchering is not that "big" a problem. Many hunters who butcher all their other wild game often balk at performing the same job on a deer. Usually it's because they are intimidated by misconceptions as to the actual size of whitetail deer. They look at a deer hanging seven feet tall on the camp pole and wonder how on earth they're ever going to stuff that monster into the freezer back home. Ah, the problems of the successful hunter!

Differences Between Beef and Venison Butchering

Another factor that inhibits many would-be venison butcherers is the greatly hyped complexity of beef butchering. At the supermarket, you can buy New York strip steaks, Porterhouse steaks, T-bone steaks, filet mignon, short ribs, standing ribs, chuck ribs, and so on; the list of possibilities is very long. That list ends with ground beef patties, which is about the only item that most of us non-professionals can cope with and understand. A beef cow, being many times larger than a deer, does in fact contain possibilities for many more exotically named (and therefore more marketable) cuts of choice meat. But again, the factor of relative size needs to be considered. Both cattle and deer have the same muscles, and it is solely these muscles that produce all the meat. (Except for the liver, there is no meat on either animal that is not considered to be muscle.)

So although there is the equivalent of a Porterhouse steak or any other beef cut somewhere on a deer, it is considerably smaller, and we end up calling it simply another venison steak rather than something more fancy. I suppose we could make venison butchering a lot more complicated if we tried to, but because we don't need to involve ourselves with the advertising and merchandising of meat products, let's keep it simple.

On a deer carcass, there are three different steaks (tenderloin, sirloin, and round) and three different roasts (neck, shoulder, and rump). That's it. Each comes from a distinctly different region of the deer. Anything that doesn't fit in those six categories will be used for stew meat or ground burger. So don't worry about the chances of ruining a deer carcass through ignorance of beef terminologies. In venison butchering, you eat your own mistakes, and no one, including you, ever knows the difference.

There is, however, one notable exception to that. All fat must be removed from venison during butchering, or the meat will not preserve well in freezer storage and will further have a tainted, waxy flavor after cooking. The so-called fat on whitetail deer is actually a tallow substance which has a higher melting point than beef fat does. Consequently, venison tallow is slow to melt during cooking and quick to congeal on your plate during mealtime. These little buttons of wax soon coat your teeth and palate and are probably responsible for the hundreds of thousands of people who had venison once and never tried it again.

Commercial butchers are prone to omit this step, often because they are still operating with beef butchering methods. Beef fat (suet) is an important source of flavor in a well-marbled beef steak, and when a butcher is selling meat by the pound, he naturally wants to leave as much fat as possible on each cut. Trimming fat off a carcass also requires more time and effort, thereby reducing the ultimate profit margin. Most commercial butchers process deer by running them quickly through the band saw blades while someone stands nearby to wrap up the pieces, bone, fat, and all. Some outfits do attempt to remove the fat, but none do as good a job as you would for yourself. The bone marrow in venison also contains tallow, which oozes out of the bones during cooking. The upshot of all this is that, if you want good, tasty venison, your best bet is to use the boneless butchering technique and to do the job yourself.

The results will be steaks and roasts cut just the way you want them, and you will have saved money too. Most commercial butchers charge twenty to thirty dollars plus the hide for cutting and wrapping a deer. The hide itself is worth at least five dollars at most taxidermists' shops, and that money might as well be going towards a new box of deer ammo rather than into someone else's pocket.

A Quick Rehash of Aging and Skinning Procedures

The tenderness of venison can often be improved by aging. Generally, the corn-fed two- and three year-old deer that comprise the majority of the annual kill are sufficiently tender so that no aging is required. These deer can be butchered and freezer-wrapped on the same day that they are dragged from the woods. On the other hand, a rugged old trophy buck weighing more than 150 pounds should probably be aged for a few days at cool temperature. Aging is a chemical process in which certain enzymes partially break down the cellular walls and fibers of meat. This process speeds up at higher temperatures so that a deer carcass will age considerably more rapidly at 40°F. than at 36°F.

Removing the skin aids in the aging process and also permits the surface of the meat to dry into a protective layer that inhibits infiltration by airborne bacteria. A deer can be conveniently aged in quarters, the cutting of which is shown in this chapter. Because most homes these days don't come equipped with walk-in meat lockers, the length of time that venison is aged will be dependant upon the weather. Sub-freezing temperatures require that the quarters be hung somewhere in the attic or an attached garage where there is sufficient household heat to prevent actual freezing. If the weather changes and the temperature averages above 40°F., it's best to proceed with the final cutting and wrapping before serious spoilage can begin.

The skinning of a deer is most easily done while the carcass is still warm, within half a day's time of the kill. Hang the deer upright, by the antlers. This positioning will later facilitate removal of the hindquarters. Remove all four lower legs with a hacksaw or an ordinary carpenter's saw and then use a hunting knife to cut the skin on the underside of each leg. Extend these cuts along the "inseams" until you reach the cavity left by field dressing. Now slide the knife between the skin and breastbone and cut all the way to the jaw. Then, with one last cut around the base of the head, the skin can be peeled down off the carcass with a little tugging here and there.

A slightly different technique is required for skinning if your deer is a trophy buck that you intend having mounted. If possible, take the entire deer to the taxidermist and have him remove the cape and head. Otherwise, do it yourself by eliminating the cut up the throat and replacing it instead with a cut up the back of the neck. This way, the mounted trophy will not have an obvious seam from chin to brisket. Be sure to include a generous cape of skin from around the shoulders. The taxidermist later can always trim off any surplus, but he can't conveniently replace missing parts.

If you instead plan to sell the whole skin (removed as described earlier), do it before the hide gets a chance to dry out and get stiff. Hides are worth more when they are still pliable and firmly holding hair. Should you delay a few days and then discover that tufts of hair can be plucked from the hide, you have waited too long and the hide is a candidate for the garbage pail. Either sell the hide while it is still fresh or temporarily preserve it by rubbing in a generous application of salt. If you salt the hide, roll it up flesh-side in and store in a cool place. This usually means in the refrigerator, and that's always good for at least one shriek from the cook unless you use a plastic garbage bag for camouflage.

The first stages of butchering can begin once the carcass has been skinned. All shot-damaged flesh should be removed and discarded. Some of the tallow can also be trimmed off at this point, but you are usually better off waiting until the carcass has been quartered into smaller portions which can be handled more easily.

Although there are as many different ways to butcher a deer as there are variations in big buck stories, the following boneless butchering method is perhaps the best for the average hunter who lacks both the space and specialty tools required for more complex attempts at butchering. All you need is a hunting knife, a standard crosscut or carpenter's saw, and some sort of wood surface on which you can cut the meat without marking up the table. A three-by-three section of plywood will serve this function just as well as the finest butchering block. An electric knife comes in handy for slicing steaks into uniform portions, but it is not truly necessary. The world had steaks long before electricity was discovered.

There are two separate stages to this boneless butchering method. First, you dismantle the carcass into quarters, as is shown. Following that, the individual quarters can be hauled into the kitchen for the final steps of cutting and wrapping. You might prefer to perform the butchering in two separate sessions in order to make the fun last a little longer. However, with a little practice, you should be able to completely butcher a skinned deer within two or three hours.

Illustrated Boneless Venison Butchering

STEP 1

The two tenderloins are located parallel to the spine, exposed to the inside of the abdominal cavity. Each tenderloin is about twelve inches long and two inches thick. Make a cut at each end and then slip your hand in and around one of the loins. Gently pry this choice piece of meat away from the spine. Remove the second loin the same way. Ideally, you will perform this step within a few hours of the kill, because the exposed tenderloin will spoil more rapidly than the rest of the carcass.

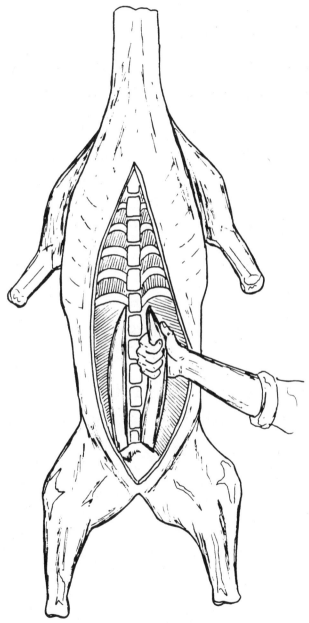

Fig. 27. *Step 1*

STEP 2

The sirloins are two huge muscles that extend the full length of a deer's back, one on each side of the spine. Peel back the tough outer membrane that conceals the sirloins. Insert the knife blade straight in along one side of the ridge of the spine and extend this cut from shoulder to hips.

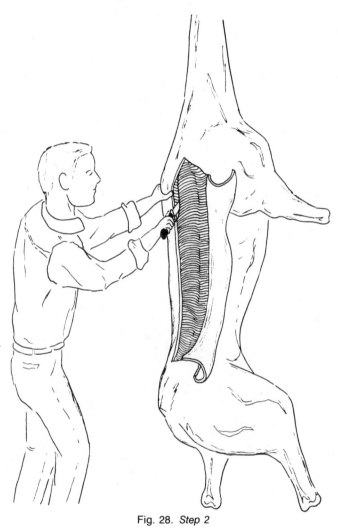

Fig. 28. *Step 2*

STEP 3

Carefully separate this first sirloin from its attachments to the ribs, making small cuts here and there as required. The sirloins are very tender and will rip if you pull too hard. Repeat both steps 2 and 3 to remove the other sirloin. Once the two sirloins are removed from the carcass, they can be sliced into small steaks or be rolled and tied with string into fork-tender roasts. If you choose the latter, first trim off a thin membrane that covers the top surface of each loin.

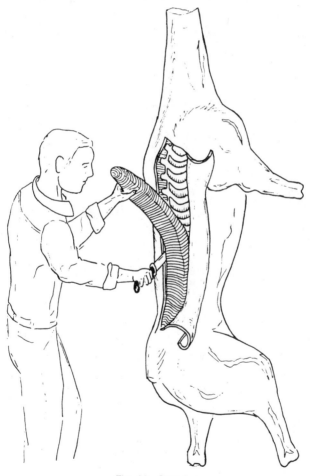

Fig. 29. *Step 3*

STEP 4

For the two neck roasts, use the same method you used for removing the sirloins. First cut straight into the neck along one side of the spine, from the base of the skull down to the first rib. Work this slab-like muscle off the spine and then cut it loose from that side of the neck. There is no meat on the front of the throat, just the windpipe and gullet. Now use this same technique for the neck roast on the other side.

Some hunters prefer to include the neck in with other scraps of venison to be used as burger or stew meat. However, if marinated or tenderized in other ways, this portion can be enjoyed as a tasty roast.

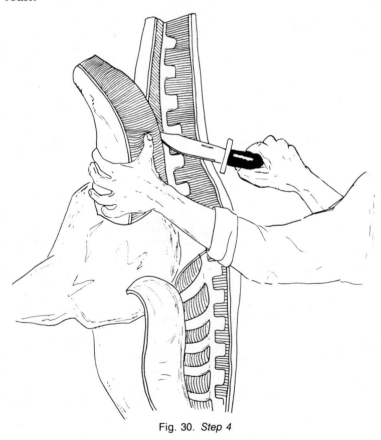

Fig. 30. *Step 4*

STEP 5

Trace the outline of one shoulder with a cut one inch deep. Flexing the leg will reveal the outline of the shoulder under the thin layers of "shrug" muscle.

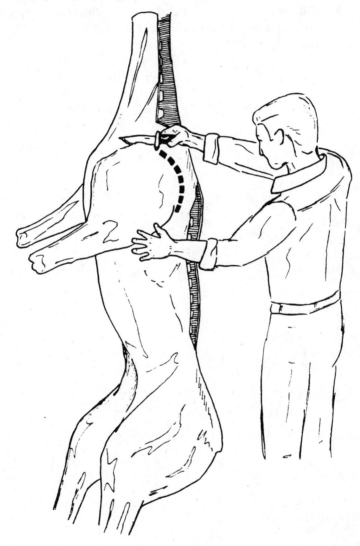

Fig. 31. *Step 5*

STEP 6

After cutting, pull the leg out sideways from the carcass and slice
through the underlying membranes. There is no shoulder ball-and-
socket joint to contend with (deer don't have them), so the entire
portion will now come free of the carcass. Do the other shoulder
the same way. For temporary hanging, cut a slit under the elbow
tendon and suspend from a nail.

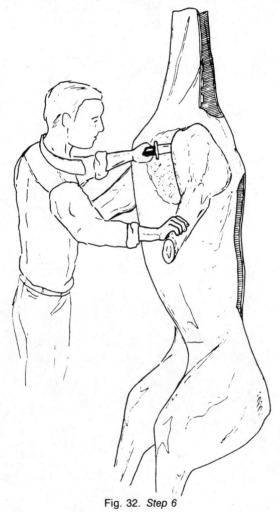

Fig. 32. *Step 6*

STEP 7

Using a carpenter's saw *upside down,* split the spine from tail bone up to just above the hips, and then from this point use a knife to cut around both sides of the waist to the belly.

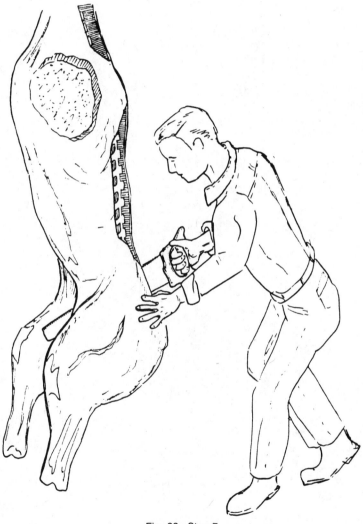

Fig. 33. *Step 7*

STEP 8

Grasp one hind leg, then lift up and backwards to break the haunch free of the carcass. The other haunch will come off just as easily. Hang both haunches (if you wish) the same way you did the shoulders. You can cut these up later.

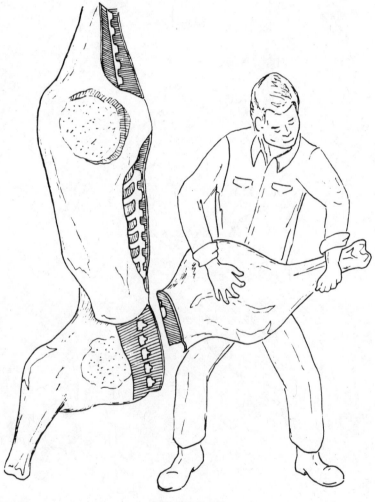

Fig. 34. *Step 8*

STEP 9

Now you can conveniently remove the various select cuts from each of the four quarters, beginning with the shoulders. The bone structure within each of the shoulders is shaped like an "L," ending at the top end with a flat shoulder blade. An excellent roast can be removed from the inside of the "L." Begin with a deep cut at the point of the elbow. Extend this cut until you hit the bone. Now check Step 10 before proceeding.

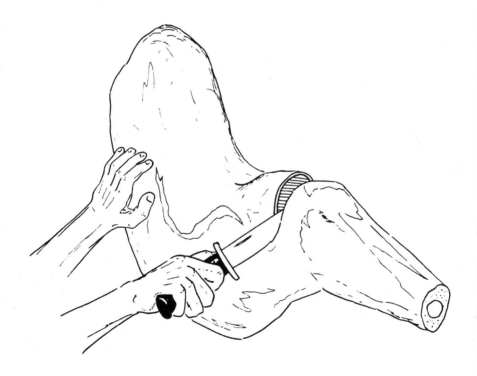

Fig. 35. *Step 9*

STEP 10

Continue cutting along the bone. Once you have determined the direction that the bone follows, you can extend the cut over and slightly past the bone so that additional venison will remain attached to the shoulder roast. After the roast is cut free, it can be rolled and tied with twine. Smaller scraps of shoulder meat can be tucked into this roast, but the tough muscles of the lower leg should be used only for burger or stew meat. Slice these muscles several times across the grain and then trim off the bone. Repeat this procedure with the other shoulder.

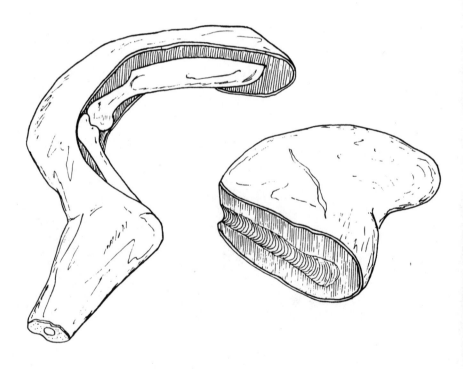

Fig. 36. *Step 10*

STEP 11

On each haunch there are two large muscles, one in front of the thigh bone and one behind it. These can be sliced into tender round steaks. First make a very shallow cut through the outer membrane, following a white fatty line that extends up the side of the thigh. This will partially separate the two muscles.

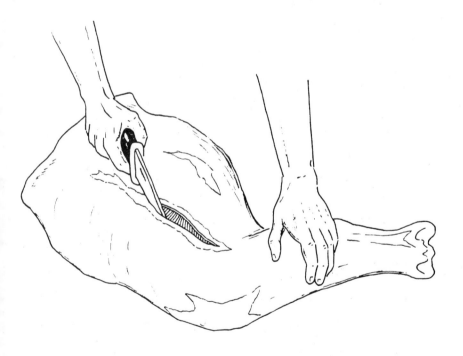

Fig. 37. *Step 11*

STEP 12

Make two deep cuts to the bone, one all the way around the top of the knee, and the other one at the hip where it folds slightly when you lift the leg. Probe these cuts to find the thigh bone and then cut the front muscle free of this bone. Slice into steaks about three-quarters of an inch thick or keep as a whole roast.

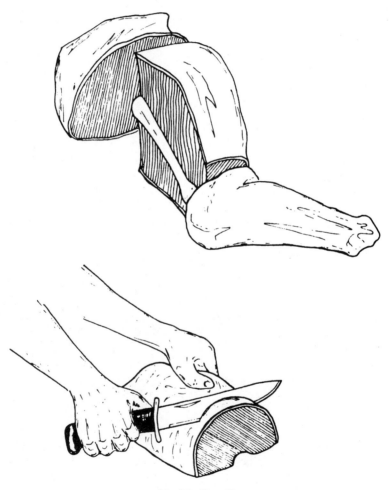

Fig. 38. *Step 12*

STEP 13

Remove the rear muscle as in Step 12. However, this muscle is more firmly attached to the thighbone, and a little extra trimming is required here. It can be used either for steaks or as a very large roast.

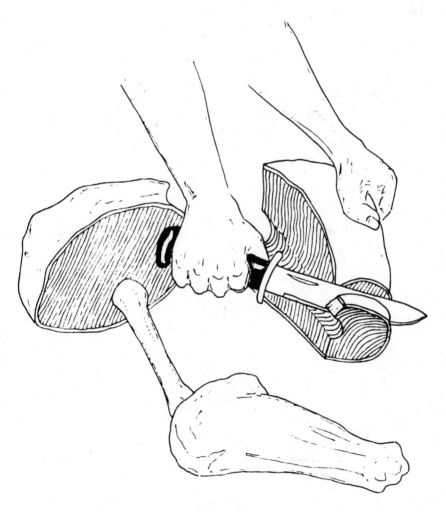

Fig. 39. *Step 13*

STEP 14

A portion of meat on the upper hip will have remained attached to the spine and hip joint. This is the rump roast, which is especially tender. Cut deeply along the spine to remove, then roll and tie. Use the lower calf muscle for burger or stew meat. The other haunch now awaits your sharpened skills.

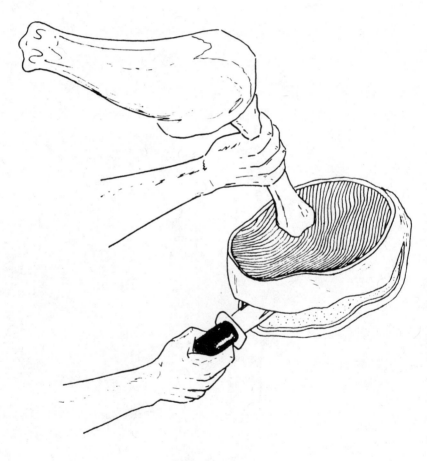

Fig. 40. *Step 14*

STEP 15

There now are less than ten pounds of venison on the carcass which has been reduced to a rib cage and spine. This remaining venison often is so laced with tallow that it is worthless. On many deer, however, these trimmings should be saved for stew meat or burger. Cut off the flanks and trim between the ribs. Add these scraps to the meat from the lower legs. Most commercial butchers will grind this into burger for a small fee. Blend with 25 percent pork or fatty beef so it will hold together.

For easy disposal of the carcass, saw off the neck and place it, along with the leg bones, inside the rib cage. The entire remains will now fit neatly inside a thirty-inch gallon plastic trash bag.

Securely wrap the roasts and steaks with freezer paper and identify each package with a felt tip pen. There should be two tenderloins for broiling, two neck roasts, two shoulder roasts, and two rump roasts. You will also have about ten servings of sirloin steaks and nearly thirty servings of round steaks. Venison is best eaten when not overcooked. Always serve hot, rare to medium. Most venison roasts are perfect after one hour at 350°F.

Fig. 41. *Step 15*

Chapter 7

What to Do with All That Venison—And How

Steaks or Stew: Increasing the Value of Venison

The portions into which a deer carcass is butchered for consumption will determine the subsequent value of the venison. It's a simple steaks-or-stew formula; a steak is worth more than stew meat if you buy it in a meat market, and the same comparison is valid in venison butchering. You wouldn't grind a beef filet mignon into burger, so why make that same mistake with venison? Too often, the decision is made to simply have an entire carcass ground up into venison burger or sausage. What a waste of all those delectably tender sirloins, roasts, tenderloins, and round steaks! Venison burger is good, that's true, but burger or sausage served in any form has never been a wholly adequate culinary substitute for a recognizable cut of meat.

Venison sausage also can be mighty tasty. But do you really need up to a hundred pounds or more of breakfast sausage for the coming year? Maybe not. Too often, if the blend of those expensive spices turns out to be not exactly to your liking, the sausage somehow gets pushed to the rear of the freezer. There it will remain, gathering frost and losing flavor until it is older than many of the neighborhood dogs. Lots of people end up giving their venison sausage away; it's the most passed around of all the venison bounty usually because there's just so very much of it, probably too much.

A certain amount of planning should be done prior to the actual butchering so you get the cuts you and your family will most enjoy. The boneless butchering techniques described in chapter 6 permit a great deal of flexibility in the final selection of meat cuts that can be obtained. For example, instead of slicing the haunches into round steaks, you might instead opt to keep these massive hunks of meat intact for a summertime roasting and basting on a spit. Rather than roll a shoulder chuck roast, another option lets you slice these smaller muscles into thin breakfast blade steaks that go very well with eggs, toast, and coffee. Ironically, when venison is prepared as burger, additional effort and expense need to be put into the venison. First, there is the cost of having the meat ground (or the effort, if you do it yourself), and secondly there is the added cost of the ground pork or beef that must be added and blended with the venison so that the burgers won't fall apart during cooking. Sausage is an even more expensive proposition because of the spices that are used. Still, there are certain portions of venison on a carcass, such as the shanks (lower legs) and flank, that are more suited for use as burger, sausage, or stew meat because of their relative lack of tenderness. The value of these portions is, by the way, increased somewhat by using them as stew meat rather than burger. As stew meat, the venison can be served in fancier meals and in a greater variety of recipes ranging from homemade stew to Stroganoff. The stew meat route is also more economical because grinding and the addition of pork or beef are not necessary.

The only way that venison loses all its value is if no one will eat it. If most of the family likes burger or stew and doesn't give a hoot for roasts and steaks, then you have to give in and put a greater portion of the deer into the form in which it will be most readily consumed.

The accompanying table shows a listing of venison cuts placed in the order of increasing toughness. At the top of this list are the most tender portions, the tenderloins and sirloins. They are also the most delectable venison cuts and therefore have the greatest value. You would have to pay a good price at the supermarket to replace them with beef cuts having comparable quality and desirability. It would be a real shame to waste the tenderloins and sirloins by using them as anything except steaks or roasts.

The rump roast is ranked in third place for tenderness, and because of its irregular shape it cannot easily be cut into steaks. That is just as well because the rump is probably the choicest of venison roasts, because of its interesting texture, and deserves being treated as such.

In fourth place is the round venison, which comes from the rear haunches of a deer. This portion of the deer represents the largest mass of meat available from a carcass (about 40 percent of the total weight of venison), and it is at this point on the tenderness list that the impact of the steaks-or-stew decision literally carries the most weight. But fear not: there are several options. Although many people put the entire haunches into round steaks, others use part of the round venison for roasts. Still others take the option of using much of the round for stew meat, burger, and sausage, although the gourmet value is lost when this is done. The word "round" is used in both venison and beef butchering to describe this region of a carcass because the steaks cut from it are "round" like a circle. Venison round steaks are fairly tender and definitely flavorsome, and there is an ample supply of these potentially valuable cuts on a deer. Whichever cut or processing you ultimately decide to apply to the venison round, you will get a good eating meat. In terms of dollar value, however, you get the most from your hunting investment if you select steaks or a combination of steaks and roasts from the venison round.

In the bottom half of the list are the shoulder, neck, shank, and flank portions. Note that these add up to 40 percent of the total edible weight of a deer carcass, which provides an ample quantity of meat for the stew or burger category. However, if the neck and shoulder portions are instead kept for serving as roasts, the remaining share of meat drops down to 15 percent. Whether or not to do this is a hard decision, but at least that decision will be made based upon good planning rather than happenstance.

The full details of butchering, including where the various cuts are located on the carcass and how they can be easily removed, are covered in chapter 6. At this point, however, it is not necessary to know all those details. Instead, use the accompanying table to first determine the choices that are available. Use the "Approximate Per-

VENISON TENDERNESS CHART FOR SELECTION OF CHOICE CUTS AND GROUND MEAT

Name	Tenderness	Approx. Percent of Total Weight	Preferred Cuts (Best Value)	Source (See chapter 6)
1. Tenderloins	Most tender	5%	Filet mignon	under lower spine (inside abdominal cavity)
2. Sirloins		10%	Sirloin steaks Loin roasts	beside spine, from hip to shoulder
3. Rump		5%	Rump roasts	top of rump, near tail
4. Round		40%	Round steaks Round roasts	haunches, between hip and knee
5. Shoulder		15%	Chuck roast Blade steak Stew or burger	both sides of shoulder blade
6. Neck		10%	Neck roasts Stew or burger	neck to tip of shoulders
7. Shank		5%	Stew or burger	lower legs
8. Flank	Least tender	10%	Stew or burger	belly and sides and from between ribs

(Venison cuts from the top of this list are most tender and get progressively less tender towards the bottom of the list. If the decision is made to put part of a deer carcass into burger or stew meat, start at the bottom of the list and work upwards until you have the amount, or total percentage, that you want.)

cent of Total Edible Weight" column to roughly compute what share of a total deer carcass you want to have in steaks, in roasts, or whatever. For example, the sum of percentages represented by the tenderloins, sirloins, and the round is 5 percent plus 10 percent plus 40 percent, which equals 55 percent. This means that 55 percent, more than half the edible weight, can be enjoyed as steaks.

How to Determine Whether Venison Will Be Tender

A fellow deer hunter, a friend of mine who possesses considerable woods-savvy, once remarked to me that the buck he had dropped the day before was really going to be tough eating. When I asked why he thought so, he replied that the buck didn't have any upper front teeth so it must have been a "tough old critter." Apparently because my friend had lost some of his own teeth with age, he figured that the buck was just as tough and old as he was! Well, the fact of the matter is that deer don't have upper front teeth; none of 'em do. Deer instead have a rubbery pad on the forward end of the upper gum that serves virtually as a cutting board for the lower front teeth. With this type of oral equipment, browsing deer can more easily slip off the bark and buds from low-hanging branches.

For one reason or another, we might suspect that a deer we are about to butcher and preserve is truly one of those tough old bucks of lies and legends. Most venison is tender, but some deer do, sure enough, produce tough meat, especially if they are old or were pushed long and hard just before the kill. If a deer does promise to be tough eating, there are certain things that can be done to improve the venison. For example, the meat aging period can be extended so that additional tenderizing is achieved. During butchering, a greater share of the venison can be earmarked for burger, sausage, or stew meat, with less remaining for steaks and roasts. But how do you first determine whether a deer might be tough? Judging age from the size of the antlers can give highly unreliable indications because bucks usually develop their best and biggest racks during the prime of life, not in the later years. Carcass weight also is not of much use in estimating age because the growth rate of most deer begins to level off soon after maturity. There are exceptions, of course, but a large one-hundred eighty eight-point buck could be any age between 3½ and a dozen years or more. Diet and environment have more effect on antler growth and body weight than do years of age. An experienced wildlife biologist can accurately determine a buck's age by examining wear on the molars. But, even if we do know exactly how old a deer is, that piece of information does not really tell us for certain whether or not the venison is going to be tough.

There is only one totally reliable way to find out, and that is to *eat* some of the deer! Sounds almost too easy, doesn't it? If the skin is still on the carcass, you nevertheless can obtain a slice of venison round steak from just underneath the exposed surface of the split haunches. Remember that the tenderloins and sirloins (see chapter 6 for locations) will probably be tender regardless what the rest of the carcass is because these muscles never receive much exercise. A small piece of round steak from the haunches will usually provide the best indicator of the overall tenderness or toughness of the deer.

Venison, like any other red meat, is most tender when it is raw. That is a fact, the truth of which is apparently appreciated only by people who prefer their steaks broiled rare or medium-rare. Of course, pressure-cooking and stewing will eventually tenderize meat beyond recognizability, but during broiling or roasting meat only gets tougher the longer it is cooked; remember this as you examine the sample wedge of venison. Either fry your "specimen" or grill it on a fork held over a flame on the kitchen stove. After cooking, test the venison with an ordinary steak knife, and then pop it in your mouth and chew it. If you have selected a piece of the haunch (round steak) for this experiment, the meat should be slightly firm but still be a pleasure to eat. The venison might seem too tough and, if it does, you should cut another sample to try before you make a hasty decision to put the deer all into burger.

The different cuts on a deer will have varying degrees of tenderness or toughness, depending on their location on the carcass. The following guidelines are based on venison from a typical, tender young buck, broiled to medium-rare. The *tenderloins* should be extremely tender, although somewhat stringy, and you should be able to cut them with a fork. The *sirloins* have an interestingly short-grained texture, whether served as steaks or as a roast, and can easily be cut with a dull butter knife. The *round steaks* yield best to a sharp steak knife but should cut with little effort. The *rump roast* is another butter knife candidate, but the *shoulder and neck roasts* respond only to a steak knife. The *shank* meat is actually too tough to be suitably cooked in any form other than burger or stew meat, regardless of how tender the rest of the buck might be.

The Biochemistry of the Meat Aging Process

Whether or not venison should be aged to achieve improved tenderness is a question that has several possible answers. Very often, the prolonged aging of a deer carcass simply isn't necessary; the majority of deer that are harvested from today's scientifically managed herds tend to be young and tender, averaging only 1½–2½ years old. Particularly, if these deer have been living around farming regions and small woodlots, where the daily search for food is neither stressful nor requiring much physical effort, the venison they produce is likely to be tender; that is, tender compared to that of the tough older bucks and to deer of any age that live in deeply wooded, mountainous regions where the constant search for a meager browse supply tends to build tough stringy muscles. But this is only part of the story; there are other factors that should still be considered.

Vension, like any other red meat, is reasonably tender shortly after the kill, but certain chemical reactions soon begin which cause the meat to temporarily toughen. This is called *rigor mortis,* a stiffening of the muscle fiber that reaches its peak within twenty-four to thirty-six hours, depending on the temperature. If a deer is butchered at this time, and the portions are quickly frozen, the venison will still be fairly stiff and tough when later thawed for cooking. (That is, the meat will be tougher than it might otherwise have been if handled differently. It might still be good and tender, but not quite as good nor quite as tender as if the deer had been aged even half a day longer.) In other words, don't butcher deer during the short period of *rigor mortis,* if you can avoid it.

The loss of tenderness associated with *rigor mortis* is gradually reversed during subsequent aging. Natural enzymes that are already in the meat do the work of the aging process. Enzymes are a form of chemical protein, and they gradually break down the connective tissues around each cell. This process has been likened to "partial digestion," and the reactions which take place within the meat are very similar to those caused by commercial enzyme meat tenderizers.

The end product of meat aging would be gelatin if aging could proceed unhindered by bacterial action. For about every 8°F. above freezing, the enzyme tenderizing action is doubled, as the following table shows.

Meat Aging Time (Days)	Temperature (°F.)
12	32
6	40
4	48
2	56

This means that, for example, venison aged for six days at 40°F. will be just as tender as if it had been aged for twelve days at 32°F. Temperature is obviously very important in aging.

The problem with aging at warmer temperatures, however, is that yeasts, molds, and bacteria on the surface of meat may develop at a greater rate. Their presence is not needed for proper aging, and they often produce an undesired rancid flavor in the meat. This gives the results of meat aging some bad names, of which "rotten" is the most common. Fortunately, the effects of these unwanted helpers can be removed by brushing the meat with a vinegar-soaked cloth and by trimming away the outer meat surface when final cutting is done.

During aging, it is important to maintain a reasonably uniform temperature and good ventilation where the venison is hung. Most homes these days don't come equipped with walk-in coolers (if they ever did), so the best compromise is usually an unheated attic or closed garage, where the extremes of day and night outdoor temperatures will be moderated into a better "average" temperature for aging. Protect the carcass (or the quartered sections) from direct sunlight and freezing winds. Measure the carcass temperature, preferably with a thermometer inserted into the venison, and check it periodically. Remember that the temperature of the carcass will fluctuate at a slower and lesser degree than will the storage room or outdoor temperature because the passage of time is required for heat to be lost or gained. Often, during the cold weather that usually accompanies the deer season, there can be a problem in keeping the venison from freezing rock hard. While this in itself is not particularly harmful to the meat, the subsequently long period of warmer temperatures required to thaw out the critter can often extend well beyond acceptable aging times. You see, the outside of the deer will be thawed (and be aging) while the interior regions are still frozen. And let me tell you, butchering a frozen deer is no fun. If you place half a pail of water near a carcass that is in danger of freezing, this can be used as an indicator of what is happening deep within the venison. Obviously, if the water doesn't freeze solid, neither will the carcass, regardless of what the outdoor temperatures reach. Nevertheless, be prepared to do a spur-of-the-moment butchering job if the weather turns excessively hot or cold.

Keep in mind that it isn't necessary to age an entire deer carcass. The sirloins and tenderloins are already naturally tender and simply don't need to be aged at all. Other portions of the deer that will be used for burger, sausage, or stew meat also can bypass aging. Generally, this means that only the shoulders and haunches (which usually will be broiled or roasted as steaks and roasts) are worth the extra effort involved in aging. These quarters can be removed from the carcass, using techniques described in chapter 6, and thus become more convenient for handling and hanging during the aging process.

There is also another important aspect of meat aging that should be understood. Meat needs to be hung in such a way that most or all of the muscles in the carcass are mildly stretched, in order to prevent shrinkage and to promote the tenderizing actions of aging. When a muscle is free to shrink, moisture is lost and the resulting meat is apt to be less flavorful and less tender. The worst way to hang an entire deer carcass during aging is by the hind legs. This position cramps the large rump and the back of the rear leg muscles, where so many otherwise choice steaks and roasts can be found. Because this region of the deer provides about 40% of the total venison, it is important that it be treated properly. Hanging a deer head-up (by the antlers) is almost as bad because now the hind legs are pulled downward by gravity, again causing those major muscles to cramp and shrink.

There are two hanging methods by which this can be avoided. The first involves hanging the entire carcass by the pelvic bone. This head-down position permits the rear legs to hang outwardly in a more natural, stress-free position. The other method is, in some ways, even simpler. You merely quarter the deer into the two shoulders and two haunches (which you were going to do anyway, because it makes

Fig. 42. Venison shoulders and haunches hung for aging. These represent 60 percent of the total edible weight of a deer and contain most of the steaks.

everything easier to handle) and hang the quarters. Cut a slit behind the larger tendons and hang each quarter on a nail. The muscles fore-and-aft of each leg bone will still try to shrink, but the effect will largely be cancelled out by the resistance of the hip and shoulder bones.

Venison should be inspected at least twice a day during the aging period. Use both your sense of touch and of smell. The surface of the meat should remain dry. As time passes, the surface will darken in color as a thin, protective casing of hardened meat forms. This can later be trimmed off. Sniff the venison up close and scrub with vinegar any area that begins to smell tainted. Unless your deer is obviously a tough old beast, don't stretch your luck with too long an aging period. As mentioned earlier, many, and maybe most, deer are reasonably tender even without aging. There are no firm guidelines as to how long venison should be aged, partly because temperature determines how fast the aging will progress, but also because every deer is a little different from all the others. Meat tenderness is a matter of personal preferences. Many people agree that too much tenderness detracts from the interesting qualities of a meat dish.

Rolling Roasts

Except for the large round muscles of the haunches, any portion of a deer carcass that is to be used as a roast should first be rolled. This is not entirely necessary, but rolling helps shape a portion of venison into something that can be more easily handled and more uniformily roasted. Rolling a roast is a very simple procedure; all you do is fold (or roll) the venison into the desired shape and then tie it into place with several turns of string. This little job is best done by two people; one person holds the venison while the other wraps and ties the string.

If a roast is to be marinated, then perform this step first and roll the roast later.

Unlike beef chuck or beef blade roasts, which can be pot roasted "flat" as a single large slab of meat, most venison roasts come off a deer carcass irregularly shaped and with much variation in thickness. Deer are considerably smaller than beef cattle, so there are fewer cuts that can be made in venison to attain handier roasting sizes. A venison shoulder roast, when removed from the shoulder blade, contains several different muscle groups that may fall apart from one another if not secured by rolling and tying. A venison neck roast, filleted from the bone, tapers in thickness from two or three inches all the way down to less than an inch. If roasted "as is," without rolling, venison roasts will cook unevenly. Rolling and tying a roast also provides the opportunity to include other bits of meat, such as an off-size steak or whatever, to increase the effective size of the final rolled roast. However, don't make the mistake of tucking a nice looking piece of shank muscle into an otherwise tender roast. Tough meat is tough meat, no matter what other label you may try to put on it.

At our home, we generally roll our roasts on the same evening that the deer is butchered and wrapped for freezing. Doing it this way seems to be less bother and it gets the job over-and-done-with

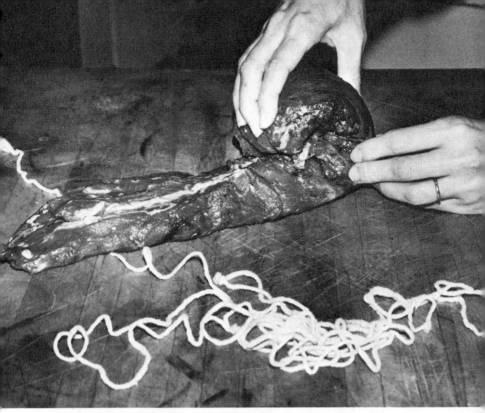

Fig. 43. Irregularly-shaped slabs of venison can be rolled and tied into compact roasts. This is a sirloin roast.

for another year. Besides, it seems that someone is always walking off with my supply of string, so I use what I've got while I can still find it. One time I delayed and had to tie roasts with sewing thread. Another roast got tied with the string from the seam of a fifty-pound bag of dog food. Obviously, nearly any kind of undyed string will do the job. The best kind, however, is a thick cotton twine that can be easily seen and removed before the venison is served.

We often smear a mustard sauce on the inner surfaces of a roast before rolling it. Various stuffings and other condiments can also be snugged-up inside a rolled roast. However, spices and most stuffings do not preserve very well in the freezer. Stuffings, in particular, are known to sometimes harbor bacterial cultures which can increase in potency during thawing. If you plan to slather a roast with

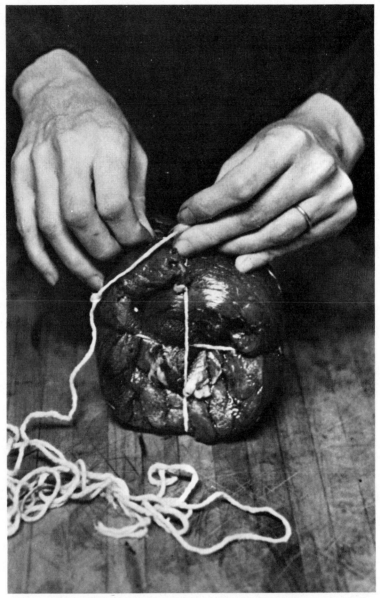

Fig. 44. The final stages of rolling a roast. Try to use a string that can easily be seen and removed before the venison is served.

any additional dressings, your best bet is to do so just prior to cooking.

Preserving by Freezing

Freezing provides the best means of preserving the fresh, natural flavor of venison. Freezing, however, also has certain limitations. You already know what most of them are. Meat gradually loses flavor over a period of time in a freezer and can even spoil or take on an undesirable "freezer taste." Frozen meat can also become freezer burned from loss of moisture through dehydration. Knowing what causes these changes to occur makes the necessary precautions seem more sensible.

First, understand that most substances and liquids do not freeze hard at 32°F. the way pure water does. Many fats and oils, water containing dissolved salts and minerals, and certain of the organic chemicals and enzymes found in meat do not freeze until much lower temperatures are attained. In fact, the meat-aging chemical reactions continue to take place, although at a much slower rate, if meat is not kept at "deep freeze" temperatures. If venison is kept for more than a couple of months at the not-very-cold 15°F. or 25°F. temperatures provided by ordinary refrigerator freezers, the quality of the flavor will begin to deteriorate, especially if the tallow has not been trimmed off. Under certain circumstances of fluctuating temperatures, even a potentially bad situation with bacterial growth can develop. Sure, we humans can appreciate a well-aged steak, but only bears, vultures, and wild dogs have a liking for rotten meat. As sportsmen (and sportswomen), we have an obligation to make the best possible use of the venison that we have rendered. This requires that we use good freezing practices to preserve our bounty. There's not much philosophical difference between wasting a deer carcass by leaving it behind in the woods and wasting a deer by throwing away spoiled venison six months later.

Most folks these days no longer buy domestic meats in very large quantities, such as in a whole side of beef or pork. The average home freezer seldom contains more than a few week's meat supply, and even these small larders are kept renewed by weekly purchase of fresh meat at the local market. Under these circumstances, there's not much opportunity to gain experience with the problems of long term meat storage. Consequently, it is often too easy to become careless with proper freezing techniques. That store-bought stuff (which seldom spends much real time in the freezer) always tastes fairly decent, so why worry, right? Well, that's the wrong attitude to have, particularly when the venison from an entire deer is being tucked away into frozen storage. Now we are talking about fifty to one hundred pounds or more of boned meat, and much of it is going to remain in the freezer for many months yet to come. No matter how you cut it (little play on words there), that's a valuable quantity of meat, and a loss of flavor would be a minor tragedy. Ironically, when venison spoils in a freezer, it is often the deer and the "gamey taste" of venison that gets blamed rather than the wrapping and freezing techniques.

Packaging and Labeling

Use a good quality polyethylene-coated white wrapping paper and apply the slick, coated side towards the meat. When wrapping, cut each piece of paper long enough to go at least two or three times around each portion of venison. Don't fold the open ends over towards the middle until after two full turns have been made. Otherwise, you would have only one thickness of paper over those ends. Secure these flaps with tape. Special freezer tape sold for this purpose supposedly does a better job of sticking at cold temperatures, but ordinary masking tape seems to work just as well, and it costs less.

Wrap packages tightly to expel pockets of air that can later permit meat dehydration and "freezer burn" to occur. If the venison is to be packaged in plastic freezer bags rather than coated paper, the excess air can be sucked out with a soda straw prior to sealing each bag. Many people prefer to double-wrap venison, and this is a good idea, particularly if the meat is likely to remain in frozen storage longer than six months. Double-wrapping usually is done using two different kinds of wrapping material. For example, a transparent cellophane or plastic wrap is first rolled tightly around the portion of venison before the somewhat looser white wrapping paper is applied. Another means of double-wrapping consists merely of dumping several single-wrapped packages into a large freezer bag

Fig. 45. The boned and trimmed venison from the average deer seldom exceeds 1½ cubic feet. Here are shown the wrapped freezer packages and stew meat representing one entire deer.

or even a plastic garbage bag and then sealing the bag after the air is expelled. The whole idea here is to minimize the gradual loss of moisture and to restrict the intrusion of unwanted flavors and odors from other foods in the freezer. Please understand that this struggle to preserve flavor is a losing battle in the long haul. With good wrapping, you gain extra months of storage time, but good flavor does not last forever. Holding frozen venison for more than a year is stretching things beyond their practical limits. Fortunately, another deer season comes along just in time. ("Whew!")

The size of a freezer package of venison should be based upon how much venison you would expect to prepare and serve at a single meal. Remember also, a venison steak that has had all the bone and tallow trimmed away will not be as large as an equivalent beef-steak with all its suet and bone still attached. Keep the portions of venison somewhat smaller than what you would serve if it were beef.

Label each freezer package with the cut of meat it contains, using a felt tip pen to avoid the punctures that otherwise could result from using a pencil or ball-point pen. You should consider putting a little more information on each label than might seem necessary at the moment. For example, if the possibility exists that there will be venison from more than one deer in the same freezer, then by all means identify which of those deer is contained within each of the packages. The opportunity to compare the meat quality of two different deer, such as an old buck and a young doe, is something that shouldn't be missed. You might want to run little side experiments, such as aging one haunch longer than the other haunch from the same deer in order to determine to your own satisfaction that aging does (or doesn't) improve venison. Without a proper label, these interesting little experiments won't prove a thing at a later date when all the packages look alike. A label should also be able to provide information to assist in the preparation of future meals. Want to later try a special marinade? If so, then select the venison cut beforehand, such as a shoulder or neck roast, and jot down the reminder to marinate on the label. There might be a certain special round or sirloin roast that looks good enough to warrant being reserved for a special occasion. Label the package accordingly. Certain slices of round and sirloin steaks are larger and better formed than others, and at our house these nicer steaks are labeled to be used during the visits of special friends and for our own weekend gourmet meals.

The smaller and ragged steaks, those that are somewhat less than perfect, are earmarked for fondue, which requires small pieces of meat anyway.

The wrapped venison should be cooled in the refrigerator before being placed in the freezer. There is a very good reason for following this guideline. If freezing is delayed by the warmth of the meat, ice crystals in the meat will grow large and sharp, puncturing the cell walls and permitting the eventual escape of moisture and flavor. Obviously, a package of meat that starts out at room temperature will take longer to freeze than one which has first been cooled. In order to obtain very small ice crystals that won't damage the venison flavor, first refrigerate the wrapped packages. Later, when you place the packages into the freezer, the meat temperature will scoot quickly under the magic threshold of 32°F. down into the freezing range.

Preserving by Canning

Canning is an alternative meat preserving method that deserves serious consideration. So much emphasis is placed on freezing as the major means of preserving meats that canning sometimes suffers under the stigma of being old-fashioned, perhaps even inefficient. The facts of the matter are that (1) canned meat will remain preserved with its flavor intact for a longer period of time than will frozen meat, and (2) canning is energy-efficient because the meat is both cooked and preserved in one fell swoop, and no additional input of energy (such as the electricity to run a freezer motor) is required.

The other side of the coin is that, if you don't have a large freezer, canning might be the only way in which the venison from a deer can be preserved for later consumption. Apartment dwellers and small families often have neither the space nor the need for a large freezer. Canning presents a very workable solution to this dilemma. Even folks who do have a freezer might prefer to can certain portions of the tougher cuts as stew meat rather than to grind it into burger or sausage.

The venison from an entire deer, assuming that the meat has been removed from the bone, can be contained within about forty quart canning jars. If only the stew meat is canned, only half a dozen jars or so are required. Whole roasts can be canned, as can cooked burgers, bulk sausage, and prepared stews. Canned venison stew meat can further be enhanced if later served as "venison Stroganoff" or if used as an addition to soups, goulashes, or chili. The list is an extensive one. With one exception, canned venison can be served as table fare in ways very similar to frozen venison. The exception is a rare steak. Canning cooks venison — and any other meat — past the point where a truly pink-in-the-middle steak is possible. However, although I personally like to see a steak on my plate be so rare that it's still half alive and nearly able to crawl off the platter, if the situation were such that I'd either have a canned venison steak or no venison steak at all, well, I guess I'd opt for a canned steak. Certainly, the soups and stews and Stroganoff that I've been served at home are case point sufficient to swing the jury with whom I live!

As was briefly described in chapter 2, all meat canning must be done with a pressure cooker-canner, because temperatures exceeding 240°F. must be maintained during canning for a period of time that depends upon your altitude above sea level. These are larger than the ordinary pressure cookers and have a sealable rim plus gauges in the lid. They are not particularly expensive, and one fact is for certain: they don't cost as much as a freezer. Yes, yes, I know that there are other ways in which food can be canned, but these no-pressure, low-temperature methods are only applicable to fruits and other high acid or high sugar foods that are naturally resistant to the growth of bacteria. And while we're on the subject of nasty things, let me also advise you to never taste canned meats until after they have been boiled for ten minutes or longer. To continue along that same vein, pressure cooking in the face of negligence is not without its potential dangers, which exist only if the directions that come with a pressure cooker-canner are not followed. Treat the stored energy of a pressurized canning vessel with the same respect and caution that you would a loaded gun. (Obviously, you already know about loaded guns or you wouldn't be reading this book.) Let's shift now to the positive side of this matter. The cost of a pressure cooker-canner and an assortment of jars and lids is considerably less than the meat value of a single deer carcass. If your situation is such that canning is the main method by which a year's supply of venison will be preserved, then the payback is in your favor. The canner will more than pay for itself the first year.

Instructions for meat canning can be found in many cookbooks and in the instructions that come with pressure cooker-canners. I will describe the fundamentals of venison canning, but I advise you to check these cooking manuals for the more specific details of the operation of *your* particular canner.

Understand first that all knives, work surfaces, and the canning jars themselves must be as clean as possible. Don't give bacteria a head start, particularly in meat canning. You may can venison that is already cooked ("hot packing") or you can begin with raw venison and perform an extra step in the canning process ("cold packing").

Hot Packing

Partially cook the roast, or brown the burger and stew meat, to the point where the venison is short of being well-done. Then pack the venison into the jars, leaving about one inch of space just below the lid. Meat shrinks somewhat during canning and you should pack it tightly into the jar, but the one inch of head space is necessary to prevent boil-over during canning. Cover the packed meat with boiling water, again leaving an inch of head space. Some folks also add a teaspoon of salt to each quart jar at this point, but it is only for flavoring, so the salt can be omitted if you wish. Wipe the rims of the jars with a clean cloth to remove any particles that might prevent a good seal and then screw on the lids. Process the jars in the pressure cooker-canner according to the directions that come with it. At altitudes near sea level, this would be at ten pounds pressure for ninety minutes.

Cold Packing

Cold packing requires an initial "cooking" step because the meat is packed into the jars while still raw. Again, remember to leave an inch of head space. Place the jars in a suspended rack in an open kettle, with the lids off, and fill the kettle with hot water to a level about two inches short of the tops of the jars. Simmer the water in the kettle for about seventy-five minutes. Then remove the jars, screw on the lids, and process in the pressure cooker-canner as described earlier in "hot packing."

Fig. 46. When packing venison in the canning jars, leave an inch of space at the top. Use only standard jars made for canning; don't use mayonnaise jars.

Spices and Other Flavorings

As mentioned earlier, the teaspoon of salt that is so automatically specified in most meat canning recipes is actually added only for flavor. The salt serves no purpose in preserving the meat, so it can be omitted if you wish. Three or four bay leaves added to each quart will do much to enhance the natural flavors of venison. Generally, however, most spices should not be included in the canning process because the intense heat and pressure of canning can cause them to become bitter. Experiment if you so desire, but it is usually best to hold back on the spicing until the venison is prepared for serving. Additions of beef suet will enrich the liquid stock for the making of gravy. Venison tallow has no value for this purpose, and beef suet substitutes for it quite nicely so that the venison cannot be found lacking. However, solid chunks of beef suet do not soften or melt during the canning process. They merely are there in the jar when it is opened and can then be diced up when the meat and stock are heated for serving. Raw suet can, of course, be shaved into smaller fragments before being added to the quart jars for canning. We have also heard good reports about using beef suet that had already been fried down into an oil before being added to the jars. There is a potential problem if too much fat is added because the slightest boil-over that takes place during canning may leave a film of grease under the lids, which will prevent a good seal. Some folks completely omit additions of fat and instead plop a beef boullion cube atop the venison before screwing on the lids.

Preparing Stew Meat for Canning

After the better steaks and roasts have been removed from a venison carcass, there still remains from 15–25 percent edible meat that is best applied to sausage, burger, or stew meat. If you have opted for stew meat and are going to can it, then plan on doing plenty of cutting. The flank and shank meat that makes up much of this portion of a deer carcass is really very tough meat. I hesitate to make such a negative statement about venison, but it's true; tough is tough, and there is no other way to say it. Prepare flank and shank meat for canning by cutting it across the grain into small chunks, the smaller the better. With the shanks (the lower portion of the legs), this cutting can be accomplished while the meat is still attached to the bone. I make all the across-the-grain cuts about half an inch apart, all the way into the bone, and then shave them off with one or two long cuts that ride parallel to the bone.

Remove all the white tallow before packing the venison chunks into the canning jars. Venison tallow has a flavor that is not very far removed from paraffin, so get rid of it. Don't let venison tallow get the chance to coat the venison and your palate with the flavor of wax.

The more tender portions of a deer, such as the haunches or the neck and shoulders, do not require the same extensive cutting in order to achieve tender morsels. These regions can merely be sliced into bite-sized chunks. Don't forget the sweetmeat between the ribs. Some hunters hack out sections of the rib cage for preparation as venison spareribs, but I usually trim this meat out as a welcome addition to the stew meat portion.

Preparing Burger for Canning

Venison burger can either be hot-packed or cold-packed, which means that it can be canned as individual cooked patties or instead as a large mass of uncooked ground meat. Ground venison is usually blended with 10 percent beef suet or 25 percent ground pork so that the end product will cling together during cooking. Pure ground venison tends to fall apart when cooked, which makes its use in a nice, thick hamburger almost impossible. If you're hot-packing, cook the burgers until they're lightly browned and then plunk them (gently) into the jars. You might first want to drain them on paper towels to keep the grease to a minimum. For cold packing, merely stuff the raw ground meat into the jars, leaving the usual one inch of head space, and process in the canner. Venison canned in this latter manner will tend to break apart during storage, but it later can be formed into burgers or meatloaf or whatever if suet or pork was added prior to canning. Some folks (purists, mainly) object to the concept of adding portions of a different type of animal meat to their venison, and that is an attitude that deserves respect. However, I have generally found that these people have not yet even tried to find out what beef suet or pork can do for venison burger. If they ever did, I believe that they would change their minds.

Preparing Roasts for Canning

There are several roasts on a venison carcass that can be neatly made to fit a quart jar with a minimum of trimming. Particularly, the smaller muscle of the haunch (the venison "bottom round"), segments of sirloin, and the shoulder roast can usually be canned intact. First, partially roast the meat in the oven to about medium doneness, if the venison is to be hot packed. I prefer hot-packing for roasts because it provides more control over how rare or well-done the venison roast will be before it meets the heat of canning. Before serving, heat the roast in an oven for a period of time no longer than what is required to warm the interior regions of the roast. Venison doesn't respond favorably to over-cooking, and a canned roast is already cooked. However, a complete second cooking (just prior to serving) is necessary if the risk of botulism is to be totally eliminated. It's your decision.

Chapter 8

Specialty Meats: The Sausages and Other Delicacies

Which Venison Cuts to Use

As we have discussed elsewhere in this book, the value of a deer carcass can be diminished or enhanced, partially depending on the ways in which we elect to process the venison. As ground burger, the economic worth of venison is probably at its lowest ebb. Of course, there is nothing wrong with putting a whole deer into burger and, in fact, many hunters' families would not consume a year's supply of venison unless it was in that form. Personal preference is always the final judge, especially at mealtimes.

The gourmet value of a deer carcass is probably best appreciated if it has been butchered chiefly into steaks and roasts. But again, for a family that is not geared to having large and extravagant meals (candles, wine, and all that stuff), the steak-and-roasts route might not be the one to follow. Venison isn't worth anything at all, of course, if it doesn't get eaten.

A third alternative, one which also increases the value of venison, is to spend a little extra time processing the venison into specialty meats. By supermarket and delicatessen standards, the price per pound of venison that has been processed into sausage, salami, bologna, jerky, smoked meat, corned meat, pickled meat, and other specialty meats will be higher than the more "ordinary" cuts. There are other advantages too. Processed meats seem to improve with age, whereas the quality of frozen meats eventually deteriorates. Processed meats are usually served in smaller portions so that the supply of it lasts for a longer period of time. And, during the processing of venison into salami, bologna, sausages and other highly appealing forms, you get to act as the virtuoso of the spice rack, inventing your own special blend of herbs and spices to get results that are the most satisfying to you.

Curing, spicing, and smoking were virtually the only techniques by which our forebearers could preserve meats for storage. Lacking freezers and modern canning technologies, they had to pour on the salt, pump in the spices, puff up the smoke, and hope for the best. Salted meat ("cured meat"), for example, was so inedible in its stored form that it had to be washed and rinsed at length to get something that tasted even remotely like meat. Today, these processing techniques are used chiefly to achieve certain distinctive flavors. While it is still true that curing, spicing, and smoking provide certain preservative qualities, these techniques should, in this modern age, be used only to augment the flavor of your venison. Sure, the processed meats can spend a longer time in the refrigerator than unprocessed meats without spoiling, but let's not stretch things too far. In fact, some folks I know keep raw, unprocessed venison in their freezers until it's time to fix up a new batch of processed meat. For some of these people, it has become tradition to convert any venison that might still remain in the freezer just prior to the upcoming hunting season into bulk sausage or whatever. Certainly, there is nothing like a pass through a meat grinder, plus a full charge of spices, to freshen up a cache of stale year-old freezer venison.

The tougher cuts of venison, the ones that ordinarily would be put into burger or stew meat, can also be utilized in sausages and in certain other processed meats such as jerky. This does not mean, of course, that the more tender portions of a deer carcass cannot also be used to create processed meats. The tough cuts are found on the lower regions of the legs and the flank meat from the lower sides and midriff. To this can be added the miscellaneous trimmings and assorted odd-size pieces that don't quite make the grade as steaks or roasts. There are a couple of pounds of tasty venison that can be obtained just by trimming the "sparerib" venison from between the ribs. If more venison is desired for processing than is provided by the cuts described thus far, then check the tenderness chart in chapter 7. This chart outlines the sequence of venison cuts in terms of relative tenderness or toughness. Start with the tough cuts and work your way towards the tender ones. All of the white tallow should be removed before the venison is cut into smaller chunks for grinding. Venison tallow (the fat) is distinctly different from beef fat and pork fat and will otherwise spoil the delicate flavor of venison that you are working so earnestly to preserve and enhance. In the place of tallow, substitute domestic fats, suet, or lard, as specified by recipe or by personal taste. There is no magic formula, no perfect proportions to determine how much domestic flesh should be added. You can, if you wish to, blend lean beef or pork in varying amounts with the venison that will be processed into sausage or luncheon meats, but all that is really needed is the fat from those domestic animals.

Bulk Sausage

The following recipe for bulk sausage was given to us by Rick and Debbie Sanders, our down-the-road neighbors, and it comes highly recommended.

SANDER'S SAUSAGE RECIPE

10 pounds venison
1 ounce black pepper
1 ounce salt
1 ounce fennel seed
1 pint cold water
1 pound bacon

The venison is ground using an ordinary hand-operated kitchen meat grinder in which a ¼″ grinder plate has been installed. The dry spices and salt are first mixed together in a bowl for uniform blending and can then be kneaded into the meat by hand. Following this, the spiced meat can either be made into patties or stuffed

Fig. 47. Bulk venison sausage is easy to make, requiring only standard kitchen spices and mixing by hand.

into casings. (Note: the preceding recipe is for mild flavor. For a hotter variety, Debbie advises the addition of one ounce of red pepper.)

That's all there is to it. You can even escape the labor of kneading the spices in by adding them instead to the chunks of meat before doing the grinding. (But, you'd miss the pleasant sensation of having all that ground meat squishing between your fingers while mixing by hand.) Some folks prefer to first add the spices to the chunks of meat and let the combination chill in the refrigerator for half a day or so. Doing it this way insures that the spices are more completely dissolved so that their flavors can soak into the venison before the grinding operation begins.

Grinding more than just a few pounds of venison with a standard hand-operated kitchen meat grinder can be a real chore. One fellow hunter told me that, after he'd ground up a whole deer by hand in a single evening, his right arm hadn't been worth much for at least two days. The arduous job of grinding wild venison can be tamed by having the work done commercially. Most custom butcherers will grind your venison for a small fee, and they can usually have the job done within a few minutes. If you figure that your own time is worth money, then the few dollars for commercial grinding is money well spent. Boned venison can be transported to the butcher's shop in a clean garbage bag. Generally, if you purchase a large cut of domestic meat, say, a pork butt roast, for blending in with the venison, the charge for grinding is waived. Just tell those good people behind the meat counter what you want, and you will usually get what you need. But remember: make certain that all the tallow and loose hair have been removed from the venison before you hand that bag over the counter. That's your job, not theirs.

Later, the ground meat can be packaged for freezing, as is, until spicing and curing can be done, or you can start the processing at once. However, spices do not survive freezing for any length of time without becoming bitter. As a rule of thumb, don't process more venison into sausage than you would expect will get eaten within three months. Keep the rest of the venison frozen until it can be used in the preparation of a new supply of processed meat.

Here's another recipe for homemade venison sausage. It's the favorite of Dave and Karin Hurlburt who, because of Dave's annual luck at deer hunting and Karin's culinary skills with wild game, both know a good venison sausage when they taste it. Their recipe calls for two parts of venison to be blended with one part of fatty pork butt roast.

THE HURLBURTS' VENISON SAUSAGE

  25 *pounds venison (2 parts)*
  13 *pounds pork (1 part)*
   5 *teaspoons pepper*
   5 *tablespoons salt*
  10 *teaspoons fennel seed*
   3 *teaspoons red pepper*
  1¼ *teaspoons sweet basil*
  1¼ *teaspoons oregano*
   5 *cups water*

The meat is cut into grind-size chunks, to which the spices and water are added and blended. The water aids in dissolving the spices so that a more complete spicing is achieved. The mixture of venison and spices is then kept overnight in the refrigerator, and ground into sausage the following day. As with the prior recipe, the end product can be used as bulk sausage or it can be stuffed into casings to make link sausage.

Casings for Stuffed Sausages

With just a few exceptions, the only real difference between loose bulk sausage and the kind of sausage that has an elongated cylindrical shape is that the latter sausage has been stuffed into a casing. Virtually any kind of bulk sausage can be "packaged" in this manner. So can korv, salami, bologna, and any other type of processed venison that has been ground into a workable consistency. There are special stuffer machines that can be purchased for this chore, or you can improvise with nearly any sort of a cone-shaped tube. One country lady of whom I've heard uses a hollow cow horn from which the sharp tip has been removed. She inserts the small open end of the cow horn into the casing and then stuffs sausage meat through the cow horn so that it fills the casing. I suspect that this same technique has been used for centuries.

And what are casings? Well, casings are the intestines of cows, sheep and pigs; that is, natural casings are. You can also buy synthetic plastic casings and "collagen" casings which are made from substances obtained from the hides of cattle. You can even sew your own casings for larger sausages from unbleached muslin. And although I have not personally had the experience of using them, it appears logical that the intestines of the whitetail deer could be similarly utilized once they have been flushed clean and given a brine cure. Natural casings come in many different sizes and types. Some are salted or brine-cured and others are air-dried. You can usually buy them at meat markets and in some delicatessens.

In this modern age, it is not really necessary to stuff meat into a casing in order to enjoy the merits of specialty meats. Tradition, more than any other factor, is the main reason that sausages and salamis and all those other types of elongated protein are made and marketed in casings. A casing is merely a container, a handy device in which in olden days a supply of preserved meat could be hung from the rafters, where it would be relatively safe from the ravages of flies, mice, dogs, small children, and other obnoxious pests. Casings also serve the purpose of presenting a greater surface area of the meat to the open air, which helps retard spoilage. Natural casings permit contained meats to be smoked since the vapors can pass through these thin membranes. In spite of these advantages, traditional and otherwise, casings presently add between ten and twenty cents to the cost of a pound of processed meat.

Making Salami

The following recipe for venison salami does not require the use of casings, yet the finished product is firmly shaped in the traditional way. The recipe itself has been passed from family to family on dog-eared scraps of paper, with small changes having been made along the way. However, the "no casing" forming method described here was invented by a fellow deer hunter, Don Levin, who has a knack for making things work better.

LEVIN'S NO CASING VENISON SALAMI

This recipe for ten pounds of smoke-flavored venison salami requires an addition of 25 percent fatty pork roast, which acts as a binder in the absence of a casing to hold the meat together. Beef could be substituted and would result in a slightly different flavor.

> 7½ *pounds ground venison*
> 2½ *pounds ground fatty pork roast*
> 10 *rounded teaspoons seasoned salt*
> 5 *teaspoons mustard seed*
> 4 *teaspoons pepper*
> 5 *teaspoons garlic salt*
> 2 *teaspoons hickory salt*
> 2-3 *ounces "Liquid Smoke"*

Blend the ground pork and venison by passing them together through the grinder a second or third time. Add the liquid smoke in two installments a couple of hours apart, working each addition in by hand.

Mix the dry spices together before adding them to the ground meat. Because this recipe does not include any water, which otherwise would help the spices dissolve into the meat, refrigerate the spiced meat for about three days. This delay gives the spices a better chance to spread their flavors and preservative qualities. On the fourth day, form the meat into rolls and then slowly bake for ten hours at a relatively cool 150°F. This time and temperature combination does the job whether the rolls are made as small size party snacks or as massive sandwich-size loafs. Ideally, the baking should be done with the salami placed on a broiler pan so that the fat can drain off, but Don Levin's experience with this has been that only a few droplets of fat are produced.

You understand, of course, that casings can be used to shape the raw meat into the traditional salami shape. However, they aren't necessary. Don has devised a method for forming uniform size rolls using a pop can and a wood plunger. Here's his method: Remove both ends of a standard twelve-ounce can. Rig a plunger by affixing a section of 2¼″ dowel to a smaller dowel and attach a similar hand grip on the other end. Stuff the raw salami meat mix into the pop can and then push it out with the plunger. This procedure works best, with fewer air gaps in the salami, if the meat is first rolled into the approximate shape of the can before it is placed into it. Larger size cans can also be used, but most of these larger sizes are made rigid by a series of grooves or corrugations which would resist your efforts to push out the meat. With a flat-walled can, the meat slides out neatly without tearing the smooth surface. When baked, rolls formed in this manner are smooth on the outside and delicious all the way through! Because the baking is done at such a low temperature and for such a long period of time, the exposed "no-casing" surface is just as moist and tender as the interior.

Italian Sausage, Bologna, and Korv

The next four sausage recipes (for Italian sausage, bologna, and both barley and potato korv) have been extensively used by Dick and Jacqueline Ropps. These nice folks are highly adept in the venison culinary arts, and yet work their miracles on a wood burning stove and with other less-than-modern devices. Nearly all of

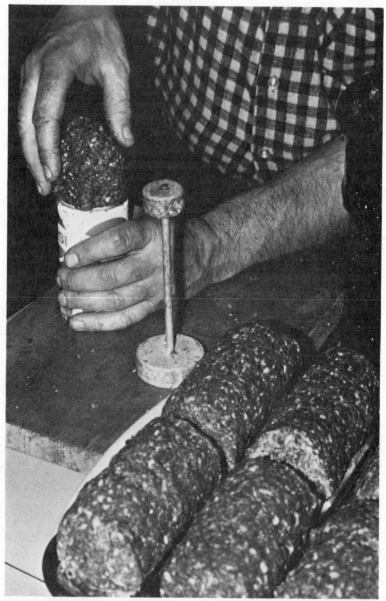

Fig. 48. "No casing" venison salami can be formed using only a soda pop can and a wood plunger.

Dick's annual venison is processed by spicing and smoking into one of the following venison delicacies.

ITALIAN SAUSAGE

> 15 *pounds venison*
> 10 *pounds pork*
> 1 *ounce fennel seed*
> 1 *ounce blacks pepper*
> 3 *ounces salt*
> 1 *ounce hot red pepper flakes*

The two meats are ground and mixed together and then the blended spices are worked into the meat. Add just enough water to make

Fig. 49. Salami rolls formed this way stay smooth on the outside and delicious all the way through when baked.

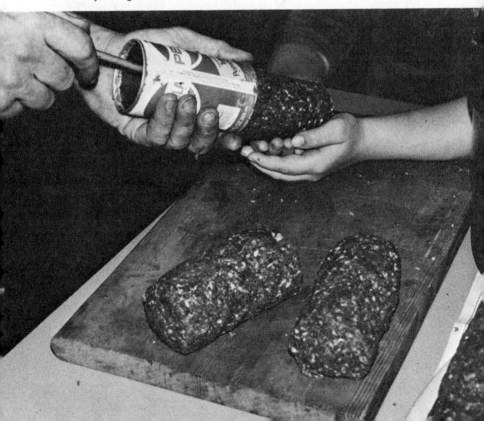

the meat moist and workable so that it can more easily be stuffed into casings. Hang the filled casings so that the sausage can air-dry.

VENISON BOLOGNA

> 25 *pounds venison*
> ½ *pound pork lard*
> 1½ *tablespoons pepper*
> 1 *tablespoon saltpeter (for color only)*
> 1¼ *pound brown sugar*

This recipe works best if the meat is seasoned before the grinding is done. Cut the venison into small chunks, mix in the blended spices, and then let the whole mass "cure" in the refrigerator for several days. Following this, grind to a fine size (preferably ⅛"), adding about one-half pound of lard during the grinding operation. Stuff into casings. The Ropps have found that plastic casings are suitable for larger size bologna sausages. The resulting sausages should then be smoked, but Jacky advises that only a brief smoking, at low temperature, is all that is required to achieve a good bologna flavor. She also has had much success with canning bologna made from this recipe.

KORV

Korv is a Scandinavian sausage that uses cereal or potatoes as a filler and a blend of spices which produce a distinct yet mild flavor. As such, korv can be used very appropriately as the meat course at suppertime without any preparation necessary except to heat it to serving temperatures in a beef boullion broth. Korv has a smooth texture and is fork-tender.

KORV (BARLEY)

> 7 *pounds venison (ground fine)*
> 4 *pounds pork shoulder (ground fine)*
> 1½ *cups barley*
> 1–2 *onions (chopped fine)*

>   2 *teaspoons pepper*
> 1½ *teaspoons ground cloves*
>   2 *teaspoons allspice*
>   3 *teaspoons salt*

The barley can be obtained in most delicatessens and in many supermarkets. Barley is packaged as a whole grain so it must first either be soaked for two hours or partially cooked before being mashed into a pulp. Blend the ingredients together by hand in a mixing container. Rinse the casings in cold water and then stuff the korv into pork casings. Many sausages do not successfully endure the rigors of freezing without loss of flavor, but korv is an exception. The use of casings is not absolutely necessary because korv can be made and served in bulk form. However, casings help retain moisture during cooking.

KORV (POTATO)

>   4 *pounds venison (ground fine)*
>   4 *pounds pork shoulder (ground fine)*
>   10 *pounds potatoes (more if desired)*
>   1 *tablespoon pepper*
> 1½ *tablespoons allspice*
>   ½ *cup salt*
>   6 *small onions, chopped fine*

Boil the potatoes until partially cooked and then mash them to a coarse texture. Then proceed as for barley korv.

Corned Meats

Corning is a form of curing by which the flavor and preservative qualities of the salts and spices are imported to the meat via a soaking process. A brine is prepared and the meat is either treated with the brine during one step of processing or is stored in the brine until eaten. Corning techniques were, until the present so-called modern age, one of the chief methods by which meats could be preserved. Today we can enjoy the special flavors of corned meats as a treat, rather than having to rely on pickled meat as standard fare.

CORNED VENISON

Corned beef and cabbage was, until recently, a very common meal. Nowadays that same meal is considered by many to be a delicacy, especially if it's made with venison. The following recipe was provided by the Ropps, and it originally called for an astonishing one hundred pounds of venison, a fact that bears testimony to the popularity of corned venison in at least one household. I have quartered the recipe to a more modest twenty-five pounds.

First prepare the pickling brine. Pickling must be done in a glass, plastic, or ceramic crock to prevent pickup of metals.

>   *1 ounce pickling spice*
> *2½ pounds salt (pickling or rock)*
>   *1 ounce saltpeter (optional, for color preservation only)*
>   *½ pound brown sugar (substitute ¼ cup molasses)*
>   *1 gallon water*

Boil all the pickling ingredients to insure a good blend and then let cool. The venison is cut into slabs about two or three inches thick. Size is not really important, but you will want to be able to conveniently handle the meat, both in the pickling and cooking stages. Rub each piece of meat with salt and then place on a supported rack, under which air can pass, for about a day. The salt will draw out the moisture in the meat and prepare it for pickling. After a day or so, rinse off the salt (which will have become soggy) and submerge the venison slabs in the pickling brine. You will probably have to weight the meat down to keep some of it from floating on the surface. The pickled ("corned") venison can be eaten within a few days, although it will keep for a long period of time if kept in the brine. How long? Well, I don't know exactly, but storage life *is* increased if the crock is kept in a cool place, preferably the refrigerator. A fermentation scum might appear on the surface, and this should be skimmed off, followed by a boiling of the pickling brine and contents for fifteen minutes. Remember that corned venison, like most other processed meats, can be canned for longer storage times. Corned venison can also be converted into "chipped" venison by smoking the meat for three or four days. This will effectively dry the venison, which can later be sliced paper-thin for serving in a white gravy.

Jerky

Most published recipes for jerky are so comparatively complicated that any newcomer to the venison culinary arts might rightfully wonder *what* jerky is! Plainly and simply put, jerky is seasoned meat that has been dried. Of course, there are many exotic ways in which the meat can be seasoned and at least three different means of drying it. But any way you do it, jerkey is still just a dehydrated chunk of meat to which various spices and salts have been added to aid in preserving the meat. Pemmican, by the way, is different from jerky because berries or other fruits with high-sugar, high-acid contents are used (rather than salt and spices) for their flavoring and preserving qualities.

Strips of jerky can be served as hors d'oeuvres, can be tucked away in the pocket of a hunting coat for nibbling upon at a future date, and can be boiled in water or in a stew over a campfire until sufficiently tender for easy and wholesome eating. If properly cured (with sufficient salt), jerky can be stored for several months in tightly lidded jars, particularly if kept in the refrigerator.

LAZY HUNTER'S JERKY

Use the more tender portions of venison, such as the haunch roundsteak or the backstrap sirloin. First slice the meat across the grain as if cutting steaks and then cut these pieces into strips about a quarter of an inch thick. This job is made easier if the venison is partially frozen. Incidentally, I have also found that the meat attached between venison ribs makes a very tasty jerky. These spareribs can easily be trimmed from the deer carcass just by slipping a knife blade along the edges of each rib. The resulting morsels are about ten to twelve inches long and are just the right thickness for making good eatin' jerky sticks.

Dip each strip in soy sauce (which is very salty) and any other spices that you might care to add. Ground peppercorns are suggested. Then place the strips on an oven tray, leaving a little space between them.

Set the tray in your oven and begin drying at about 110°F. Gradually increase the temperature to 160°F. over a six to eight hour period and then check the jerky for dryness. A strip of jerky should be brittle enough to snap in two when you try to bend it. Remember too that jerky will be more brittle after it has cooled down to room temperature; while still hot, it tends to be somewhat more pliable.

Jerky can also be dried adequately just by the heat of the sun if the weather is hot and dry, although this more natural way of accomplishing your goal might require a couple of days drying time. Jerky dried on racks near the warmth and smoke of a hardwood campfire will be particularly flavorsome.

DELUXE VENISON JERKY

This method employs a curing brine and is more suitable for making large quantities of jerky that are intended to be stored for a longer period of time. The following brine recipe is sufficient for twenty pounds of venison.

> *1 gallon water*
> *1 pound salt*
> *½ cup vinegar*
> *1 garlic clove*
> *1 ounce pickling spices*

Slice the venison into strips as described in the Lazy Hunter's method. Then soak in the brine for a week or more. Following the curing, rinse off the jerky strips and then smoke on racks for twenty-four hours. Thoroughly dried and cured jerky can be preserved literally for years if kept in a cool, dry place where air can circulate freely around the meat. But why would you want to keep something that tastes so good for *that* long?

Pickling

Pickling is probably the easiest way to process venison into a specialty meat. Because venison that has been pickled has an intense spicey and vinegary flavor, it is really suitable only for such culinary events as snacks during post-deer season football games. Pickled venison is best served as small cubes impaled on toothpicks, with adequate liquid refreshment available to balance the nips against the sips and the nourishment against the nectar. ("Honey, would you please pick those toothpicks up off the floor?")

Almost any cut of venison except the shanks can be pickled, and even the shank meat (the lower legs) could be used if you wait long enough. Vinegar, the major ingredient in the pickling solution, acts upon the venison as a marinade, tenderizing meat that might otherwise fail the chewing test.

I usually pickle only the heart and the tongue, which combine very nicely to fit just slightly less than one quart-size mayonnaise jar. Frankly, I'll admit that about three out of every five deer hunters of my acquaintance won't even talk to me about pickled tongue; they don't want to hear anything about it. But that's their problem. A whitetail buck's tongue is nearly ten inches long and two inches thick at the base, and I consider this organ to be a good-sized delicacy worth saving. The flesh from both the heart and the tongue is short-grained and relatively free of gristle, yet it remains fairly firm and tastefully textured for a long period of time in the pickling jar. The heart is removed from the deer during the chore of field dressing. There is a transparent membrane surrounding the heart which can be removed at any time before the heart is prepared for pickling, but because it serves to protect the meat like a plastic wrapper, there need be no rush to take it off early.

The tongue can be easily separated from the carcass in less than a minute. No, you don't open the deer's mouth. Instead, make a "V"-shaped incision in the soft underside of the lower jaw from the throat region to the tip of the chin. The point of the "V" should be pointed towards the chin. Reach up into this incision and pull the tongue downward and outward. You will find that it is attached only at the base of the throat where it can be cut free of the carcass.

Both the heart and tongue should be boiled for about twenty minutes to cook them in preparation for pickling. The skin on the tongue will turn white during boiling, and you might want to remove it before pickling, but this is not necessary. Slice the tongue into ⅛" thick pieces and chop the heart into small, snack-size cubes. The pickling solution is vinegar to which spices have been added. Either white or cider vinegar can be used; it makes no difference. Place the pieces of tongue and heart in a quart jar and then pour in enough

Fig. 50. Venison tongue can be boiled and then sliced for pickling. The skin turns white during cooking.

vinegar sufficient to cover all the meat. Then toss in whichever spices that appeal to you. The following recipe is more a suggestion than a recipe because the vinegar by itself will insure the preservation of the meat.

PICKLED-HEART-AND-TONGUE

2 cups vinegar
½ ounce pickling spices
1 tablespoon brown sugar
1 teaspoon peppercorns
2-3 drops red food coloring (optional)

That's all there is to it. You can begin snacking on this delicacy tomorrow, or you can wait for months. Store in the refrigerator for longest life. One of the neatest things about pickled heart-and-tongue is that you can entice folks to eat and enjoy before telling them what it is.

Smoking Venison

Like the other methods of spicing, salting, and pickling described earlier in this chapter for the processing of venison into sausages and other forms that are both flavorful and less susceptible to spoilage, smoking also provides these features. But somehow, the smoking process often seems to be one extra step requiring too much equipment or too much expertise. While it is true that the art of meat smoking is somewhat beyond the realm of the average kitchen, that does not mean that venison cannot be smoked in the average backyard using "equipment" as simple as a cardboard box or a hooded charcoal grill. Meat smoking can, of course, be made to be as complicated as your heart desires, or it can be done as easily as building a smoky campfire!

What we are looking for here is a means of imparting a smoky flavor to our sausages, jerky strips, an occasional rolled roast or "corned" venison slab, and any other hunk of tender venison that we might see fit to later slice or dice into sandwich meat. Under the usual circumstances of food smoking such as would be applied to fish and other raw meats, a brine soaking is usually required before the meat is hung in the smoker. However, sausages, jerky, and corned meats have already been "cured" by the salts and spices that were added earlier during their preparation. And, for that matter, a raw venison roast does not really need to be first cured in a salt brine if it can be properly roasted right after a one- or two-hour smoking period. However, chunks of venison that will later be sliced for cold meat sandwiches will be tastier if first cured in a seasoned brine. Use a glass, plastic, or ceramic container for the brine and soak the venison for several days at cool temperatures. A brine recipe like the one described for corned venison earlier in this chapter will suffice, and you can alter the spices to suit your fancy. Venison that has been cured before smoking will have a pleasing texture and will be more flavorsome. Incidentally, cured venison will be more apt to retain its hamlike dark red color throughout the cooking process.

The length of time that venison should be smoked depends on the thickness of the meat and the amount of smoky flavor that you want the meat to have. An entire "ham" (one whole rear haunch) might require two full days of smoking. Large two or three-inch diameter sausages require about twelve hours, but smaller sausage links, venison burger patties, small rolled roasts, and one-inch thick slabs of corned venison can be adequately smoked in less than two hours. There is an excellent book available which describes the full details of meat-smoking. It is *The Home Book of Smoke-Cooking Meat, Fish and Game,* by Jack Sleight and Raymond Hull (published by Stackpole Books). The scope of this book describes every method from the simplest to the most complex for the do-it-yourselfer.

Let's look at one simple method by which jerky and the other smaller portions of venison can be smoked in the backyard using improvised equipment. We will consider this to be merely an introduction to meat-smoking — a no-cost, low risk experiment of the kind from which we can gain some experience. Later, having tasted success, more elaborate methods can be attempted with confidence. All that is needed for this first trial run are a smudgy, smoky hardwood campfire, some yard-long stakes driven into the ground from which racks can be suspended at varying levels, and one or two large sheets of cardboard or plastic to keep the smoke from drifting away too rapidly. A charcoal grill could also be commandeered for smoking, but certain modifications would have to be jury-rigged so that the meat could be suspended no closer to the fire than eighteen inches. Our contraption should permit the meat to be flavored by the smoke without being excessively heated. There should be little or no open flame coming from the campfire. An ideal way to insure this is to start with a bed of hot charcoal upon which are placed small chunks of green, moistened hardwood. Virtually any type of hardwood can successfully be used. Even though "hickory" or "apple" sounds tastier than "locust" or "beech," the plain fact is that the average palate cannot tell the difference, especially if the meat had been cured and seasoned earlier. Use whichever type of hardwood you can get; even the green leaves from hardwood trees can be substituted. So can corncobs. But don't use pine or other coniferous woods because the bitter resins they contain will ruin the flavor of the venison.

There are at least a couple of different ways by which the venison can be supported within the rising pillar of smoke. Strips of jerky and strips of stuffed sausages can be individually hung from paperclips that have been bent into an "S" position. Long strips of jerky can simply be draped over a horizontal stick, but once they're smoked and dried this way you can't straighten them out. Roasts, larger slabs of meat, and venison burger patties are best supported by a grating, which you can either borrow from a charcoal grill or improvise from half-inch wire mesh. Ideally, the grating and its supports are fashioned in such a way that the height above the smoldering embers can be adjusted. Midway through the smoking period, turn the venison to get a more even flavoring.

Some sort of venting should be arranged at the top of your backyard smoker so that a constant upward flow of smoke can occur. Otherwise, the smoke will stagnate around the venison, allowing soot and creosote to form. In a proper smoking operation, a continual upward flow of fresh, moist smoke helps to insure that the preservative qualities (and the tasty flavors) of the organic chemicals produced during hardwood combustion are imparted to the meat.

A more detailed listing of the equipment needed for the curing and smoking of venison is given in chapter 2.

Chapter 9

Venison Cooking Tips and Recipes

The cooking of venison has, in many hunters' households and various outdoor magazine articles, and oftentimes just by word-of-mouth, been elevated to a level of an arcane art. We annually are exposed to venison recipes so complex that they each require at least half a page of fine print, involving (it seems) every spice in the rack and at least a solid afternoon of kitchen time. Under circumstances like these, it is easy to become intimidated, throw up our hands in dismay, and then either (1) get the whole deer ground up into burger in hopes that maybe someday it will get eaten, or (2) stuff neatly wrapped packages to the rear of the freezer and then forget about them until the grocery money runs low. Nationwide, the deer hunter success ratio is weighted so heavily in favor of the wily whitetail that the average hunter gets to bring home a buck only once every three or four years. As a result, culinary skills get rusty during the dry years, and venison acquires the reputation of being such an exclusive (and elusive) food that it gets treated like peacock tongues. The fact of the matter is that most of the venison on a deer can simply be fried as steaks with no preparation other than to perhaps first melt a little margarine in the pan. Let's start from that basic fact and work our way into the more complex recipes with that knowledge. We can make the preparation of venison as complicated as we desire, but we should remember to blame ourselves, rather than the whitetail deer, if the time spent in preparation does not ultimately seem worth the effort. Oftentimes, the easiest way is also the best way, with the tastiest results.

Venison Tallow vs. Other Fats

In several places throughout this book, the point is made that the white tallow (the fat) of the deer should be removed from all venison before the meat is preserved or cooked. My reasoning there is based on the fact that venison tallow is a considerably different hydrocarbon than beef and pork fats. Venison tallow is similar to a wax or a paraffin and even has a flavor not unlike these two substances. It also solidifies into little wax-like buttons soon after cooked venison has been removed from the oven or fry pan and has begun to cool. Unlike beef or pork fats, which remain juicy and liquid for a longer period of time, solidified venison tallow can soon spoil an otherwise delicious meal. Your best bet is to simply remove the tallow during butchering so that the truly good flavor of lean venison can be rightly appreciated. Venison tallow can, by the way, be turned into a very nice soap if the soapmaking methods described in chapter 11 are used.

The approximate cooling temperatures at which various cooked animal fats begin to turn from liquid oils back into solid substances are shown below.

Goose fat	88°F.
Chicken fat	90°F.
Butter fat	91°F.
Rabbit fat	95°F.
Pork lard	97°F.
Beef suet	100°F.
Mutton tallow	104°F.
Venison tallow	115°F.

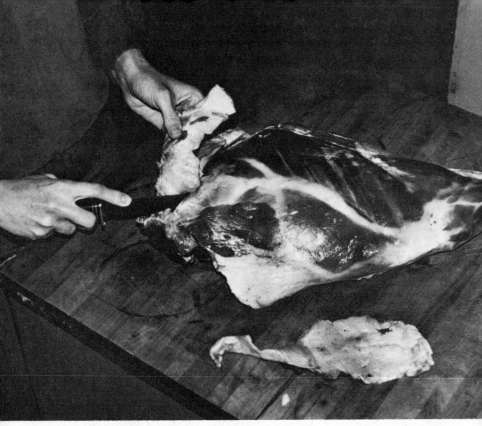

Fig. 51. The white venison tallow should be removed from all portions of edible meat and can be used for making soap.

As you can see from the preceding list, cooked venison tallow begins to harden much faster at a higher temperature than do all of the other more common animal fats. At 115°F., which is about how hot a piece of meat on your dinner plate would be within just a few minutes after being served, venison tallow will solidify into little wax buttons. Most of these little buttons will be so small that you can hardly see them, but your tongue and palate will know the difference! Even mutton tallow, which by itself has a poor reputation among gourmets (including leg-of-lamb lovers), has a solidification temperature that is well below venison tallow. Beef and pork fats, when cooling, remain juicy for a much longer period of time; so do fats of domestic fowl. If you still aren't convinced that venison tallow is devoid of any redeeming culinary qualities, then try the following kitchen experiment. Cut a piece of pure tallow into small slices and heat these in a frying pan over a low flame until the tallow has been rendered into a grease. The repugnant odor which will now fill the kitchen (and maybe even the rest of the house) should be indication enough. But if it isn't, then wait for the grease to cool and taste a bit of the stuff. (Aha, gotcha! Ugh!)

Most recipes for venison burger or sausage require the partial addition of beef or pork fat. These domestic fats serve the purpose of binding the small meat particles during the cooking process. For example, 100% pure venison burger will fall apart when it is fried. Much of the flavor of domestic meats comes from the fatty tissues, as is particularly the case with a well-marbled beefsteak. When you add domestic fats to venison, some of that domestic flavor obviously combines with the venison flavor. However, wild venison lean meat has such a sufficiently distinctive flavor that it can withstand this blending without losing all of its own character. If you do use a recipe that calls for several pounds of a beef or pork roast to be added to the concoction, remember that all you really need to add is a considerably smaller portion of beef *fat* or pork *lard*. These can ordinarily be obtained at a meat market for mere pennies a pound or sometimes even at no charge at all. The butcher will usually ask you whether the fat will be used for your consumption or for placing in a bird feeder. What you should reply (with a smile) is that any portion left over when you're done with it will be fed to the birds. Having been honest, you will be rewarded with a "no-charge" ticket — usually.

The True Taste of Venison

Before we pass this point and get deeply involved with the intricacies of the various recipes that follow, let's pause to first make an appraisal of the true taste of venison. After all, because our venison cooking techniques and spices should be intended solely to enhance the gourmet flavor, we should first have a pretty good idea of where it all begins. Look at it this way: knowing the taste of lobster, you wouldn't attempt to prepare it in a tomato sauce and thereby ruin the delicate fragrance of this natural delicacy. Similarly with venison, it should be understood that venison has a distinctive flavor which can be effectively masked or completely lost as a result of a heavy-handed assault on the spice rack. Sure, if you want to take that approach and simply use venison as a source of protein in a complicated casserole, then go right ahead and enjoy your concoction. But *please*, don't think that venison flavor is something that needs to be hidden or disguised as something else.

If a deer carcass has been properly handled and butchered, the venison will have what most people consider to be a pleasing flavor. Compared to an equivalent beef cut, venison seems to come across with a hint of herbal flavors. If pressed to be more specific, I would say that venison tastes something like beef to which a dash of freshly ground peppercorns has been added. I am tempted to include the flavors of mustard and parsley, but perhaps only because these two spices combine so well with the flavor of venison. The odor of beechnuts also comes to mind. But there is a more pronounced difference between the textures of the two meats. If you perform a direct comparison, first with a forkful of beef steak and then with a forkful of venison steak, you will quickly realize that venison is the superior meat for easier and more pleasant chewing. Beef is more coarsely textured, somewhat burlapy; so is pork, as a matter of fact. Venison is short-grained in all the regions of the sirloins and round steaks where most of the better roasts also originate. The belief on the part of some folks that a venison steak needs to be tenderized by pounding or extensive marinating is largely based on misconceptions of the true qualities of venison. Let's also consider venison from the perspective of our sense of smell, which plays a very important part in our sense of taste. Let's say that you have purchased a supermarket steak or a package of pork chops. After the cellophane has been ripped from the polystyrene tray in which meat is sold, the odor of fat is so overpowering that we don't really get a chance to know what lean beef or lean pork actually smells like. Well sure, the domestic fats do, in fact, smell very tasty, even while still raw. We have been conditioned to think so. Nowadays, however, we have learned that all that fat isn't good for us. We don't normally eat enough whole grain cereals, nor do we get enough truly rugged exercise, to justify a high fat intake. But we still get stuck with having to buy fat with the packaged meats that we bring home. With properly butchered venison, the fat (the tallow) has already been removed. So, rightly, we should compare the flavor and odor of lean venison against lean beef and lean pork because we don't eat the fat anyway. In such a comparison, I claim that venison is the only lean meat of the three that has a truly discernable identity. Venison smells good, tastes good, and is easy to chew. If a venison dish fails in any of the three preceding categories of odor, flavor, and texture, it is our fault and not the fault of venison.

Rare or Well-Done: How to Serve Venison

When possible, venison steaks or roasts should be served somewhat less cooked than you would ordinarily serve these same cuts of domestic meats. Overcooking tends to toughen venison and sometimes alters its flavor. Of course, many people prefer that their meat be cooked well-done, apparently because the thought of eating something that even remotely resembles raw flesh is repugnant to them. Be that as it may, the consequences of overcooking are still the same. Cooking causes the fluids in the meat to congeal, and it also gradually breaks down the cellular walls of the meat and permits the flavors that were contained within to escape. If you are one of those people who don't think that you'd enjoy a rare or medium-rare cooked piece of meat, I implore you to at least *try* eating a piece of venison that way. You might change your mind as a result of that little experiment.

Most beef and pork cuts can partially survive overcooking because even the leaner portions are usually well marbled with fat which melts and continues to self-baste the meat. Venison is basically a much leaner meat, and unless other fats and liquids are added during cooking (as in preparing a stew), venison will be harmed by overcooking.

Here's something else to consider. Although pork and bear meat should be cooked well-done to avoid the possibility of a trichinosis infestation, both venison and beef do not contain the types of parasites that can also inhabit the human body. From that point of view, you don't need to think of cooking as a sterilizing process when preparing either beef or venison. It's one less thing to worry about. I have even eaten occasional tidbits of totally raw venison while butchering deer in order to perform on-the-spot tenderness checks. Raw venison tastes pretty good, except that it could perhaps use a little salt. Remember that a steak or a roast is most tender when it is raw; cooking by broiling, roasting, or frying can never make meat more tender than it was originally. I'm not advocating that venison be eaten raw, but I do strongly suggest that venison should not be cooked past pink-in-the-middle. Incidentally, it is difficult to judge the degree of doneness in a venison steak or roast because venison is such a darkly colored meat. Beef and pork tend to lighten in color when cooked, but venison remains dark. To be on the safe side, remove venison from the cooking heat while it still looks to be a little on the under-done side. If closer examination indicates that more cooking is needed, you can always plop it back on the fire. But remember, hot meat will continue to cook for a while even after it has been served on a platter.

Tenderizing and Marinating

Generally speaking, most venison does not need to be tenderized before it is cooked. That's a fact. The sirloin and round steaks and the shoulder and rump roasts are usually sufficiently tender so that tenderizing by pounding, marinating, or by use of commercial meat tenderizers really isn't necessary. These cuts comprise the greater share of a deer carcass. Even a tough old buck will produce tender steaks and roasts if the venison has been sufficiently aged.

Of course, tenderness is a word of relative value, and what might be tender to one diner might be considered to be a little too chewy by another. Certainly a marinated steak has a flavor and an extra tenderness that makes the effort of tenderizing worth your time spent doing it. But don't be in a rush to add a tenderizing agent just because the wrapper says "venison." First determine which part of the deer is represented by that label.

Venison cuts that can be improved by tenderizing are the flank steaks, the lower shank muscle, and the neck roasts. (See chapter 6 for details of where these tougher cuts originate.) If these latter cuts are used for sausage or ground venison burger, then tenderizing obviously isn't needed. However, stews and certain other concoctions in which these tougher cuts can be used will be improved if the venison is first tenderized.

Marinating is probably the best way to tenderize a meat because flavoring is achieved at the same time. To be effective, the marinade solution must contain an acidic ingredient such as vinegar, tomato juice, wine, or citrus juice. Even sour cream and yogurt can be used because they both contain lactic acid as a product of bacterial action. The tenderizing effect of a marinade works best (and most rapidly) on smaller cuts of venison such as chops or steaks because a penetrating of the solution must take place within the meat in order for tough muscle fibers to be adequately broken down. Larger roasts can be marinated in a plastic bag, which serves to hold the juices against all surfaces of the meat, and will be adequately tenderized in about twenty-four hours. Smaller cuts can be marinated in a shallow bowl in just a few hours. Prick the meat occasionally with a fork to help the marinade penetrate to the inner regions.

The following marinade recipe for venison has been used often by Dick and Jacqueline Ropps.

VENISON MARINADE

¼ *cup honey*
¼ *cup lemon juice*
1 *tablespoon Worcestershire sauce*
¼ *cup cooking oil*
1 *chopped garlic clove*

You don't need a great volume of marinating solution; just turn the venison occasionally so that all surfaces remain wetted.

Serving Sizes

Usually after we are finished eating a beefsteak or a portion of pork, there will remain on our dinner plate a considerably large amount of fat, gristle, and possibly bone. Such will not be the case with venison because the venison will have been trimmed free beforehand of all this undesirable stuff. By doing our own butchering, we will have not only improved the quality of the meat, but we will also have made the portions appear smaller. This is an important fact worth remembering when serving sizes are determined. A portion of a venison roast no larger than your fist is probably more than you can comfortably eat. Similarly, a venison steak is adequate to a hungry hunter's needs at about half the size of a normal T-bone or Porterhouse. Even when served as stew meat or as something like a Stroganoff, venison seems to stretch farther than the domestic meats. Go easy on your supply of venison; it is a delicacy that shouldn't be wasted by serving in overly large portions.

Charcoaled Venison

In my opinion, the worst way to cook a venison steak is to simply plop it on a charcoal grill. This method just doesn't work; plain charcoaled venison is about as tasty as a hot suede glove. The reason for this can be better understood if we first take a look at what happens when a well-marbled beefsteak is charcoaled. As the temperature rises within a beefsteak, the fatty tissues begin to melt so that droplets of fat ooze out to drip onto the hot coals. When they do, these droplets smolder and burn, which produces a smoke that rises to flavor the beefsteak. A charcoaled beefsteak tastes good because the meat has actually been partially smoked. Venison, on the other hand, cannot produce a good smoky flavor because venison lacks both the type and the amount of fat needed for this purpose. This means that if we want to charcoal venison we must add a good flavored, fatty substance directly to the venison, something that will melt and subsequently smoke. Butter or margarine will at least get us pointed in the right direction. Place the venison steaks on the grill until the downward sides are warmed and then turn the steaks so that a dab of butter can be smeared over them. Then repeat this on the other surfaces. Continue basting until the steaks are done. This same thing can be done using beef suet that has earlier been rendered to grease in a fry pan. I have tried just placing chunks of raw beef suet on the grill alongside venison steaks, but this technique doesn't give good results. Solid suet melts too slowly at first and then too profusely a few minutes later, and in the meantime, the lean venison shrivels and dries above the hot coals.

There are, of course, many venison connoisseurs who swear by plain-and-simple charcoaling as the best (rather than the worst) way to cook a lean venison steak. What can I say? Only this: I agree that a charcoaled venison steak is better than no steak at all.

The Frying Pan Method

Many a whitetail deer has met its ultimate destiny with mankind via piecemeal passage through the open portal of a frying pan. One fellow I know uses only a frying pan to cook virtually all of each year's deer. Sure, he grinds a small portion of the tougher cuts into

Fig. 52. Venison does not charcoal very well unless other good flavored fats or oils are added to the meat.

burger, but the major share of venison that other people might put into roasts or stews and other meat dishes is instead patiently sliced into big and little frying-size steaks. The other members of his family claim to not like venison (they won't try it, and she won't cook it), but a potential domestic conflict has been averted by this fellow's willingness to do his own venison cooking, fry pan style. And he doesn't really mind; he gets to keep all that venison for himself!

Frying is a very suitable means of cooking venison because the meat can be cooked hot and fast without undue loss of moisture and tenderness. With just a dab of butter, margarine, or vegetable shortening melted into the skillet, a venison steak can quickly be turned into a first class main course. (Don't use vegetable oil; it burns at too low a temperature in a fry pan and gives venison an oily flavor.) Other flavorings, spices and sauces are really not necessary for the frying of venison steaks. However, as a point of interest, I'll add the fact that if beef suet is first fried down to a grease before the venison is plopped into the pan, the resulting steak will taste nearly identical to beef. For this purpose, chunks of beef suet can be kept in the freezer in a plastic bag, ready for your use. One drawback to frying with suet is that it smokes like the dickens, so be ready to rescue your steaks from the kitchen smog and to douse the fry pan in cold running water. By using suet, you not only get to enjoy a tasty steak, but you also get to smell it throughout the house for several hours afterwards.

There is no magic dimension to which a venison steak should be sliced. Thick or thin, venison will be tasty if it's not overcooked. The sirloins, which are somewhat small, can be butterflied into quarter-inch thick steaks that require only ninety seconds of frying on each side, and less time than that if you prefer steaks cooked less than well-done. The secret of success in frying venison steaks is to do it hot-and-fast, delaying the cooking until after everything else is on the table and ready to go. In fact, my wife Peg and I enjoy venison fresh off the griddle so much that we usually don't fry our second helpings until after the first helping has disappeared.

We ordinarily slice venison steaks about ¼" thick so that we can fry to medium rare on the inside without having to overcook the steaks on the outer surfaces. Overcooking toughens venison, remember that. A truly thick beefsteak can survive overcooking, but venison can't. If treated with a modicum of respect, heat, and speed, virtually any portion of a deer carcass except the shank and flank meat can be fried as steaks. Many of these customized steaks will admittedly be small, but you can only get just so much in your mouth at one time anyway.

If your personal preference leans towards well-done meat, then you might consider the tenderizing actions of marinating to offset the loss of tenderness that accompanies overcooking. I refuse to refer to well-done as being anything less than overcooking, at least when we are talking about venison. A wine marinade is particularly suitable for small steaks that will be pan-fried. Cover the steaks with red wine for six to ten hours. Any red wine will be sufficient, even a cheapie that has turned sour on you. Butter, margarine, or whatever will still be needed, sizzling in the pan. The only other item that improves the flavor of a pan-fried venison steak is the proper amount of hunger and anticipation.

Broiling

At this point, we dispense with the frying pan and take a look at another easy means of cooking venison steaks. Because an oven broiler operates with an open, hot flame, a venison steak can be quickly cooked without undue loss of moisture. Unlike charcoaling, which produces lower temperatures and requires longer cooking times that would dry out venison, broiling gets the job done in just a few short minutes while sealing in the juices. Whereas a fatty beefsteak in the broiler can jump into bright yellow flames that add a dash of excitement to your supper preparations, lean venison behaves itself and doesn't cause any trouble. Again, because of the absence of fat in venison, you can broil it on a small sheet of aluminum foil and escape the chore of cleaning the broiler. No fuss, no muss, just good eating. Of course, you can plunk a chunk of beef suet atop your venison steak to make it taste like beef, but doing that would only complicate matters and mask the true flavor of deer meat. Venison should be placed close to the flame, so adjust the rack in the broiler accordingly. Don't get involved in any conversations or phone calls while the steak is broiling. Just a few minutes or less on both sides is all a venison steak really needs.

Whole venison sirloins are sufficiently small enough that they also can be broiled in much the same way as a steak. The sirloins run nearly the full length of a deer's back from hip to shoulder. Venison sirloins are most often cut into smaller steaks (which some folks call the "chops") or are rolled into roasts. This prime cut can also be broiled whole if there are enough taken seats at the supper table to warrant such an extravagance. We are talking here about a piece of venison that is up to two feet long but only two or three inches thick and somewhat more wide than thick. It can be cut into shorter segments for broiling. Nothing except the sirloin itself needs to be tucked into the broiler to produce a memorable venison meal, but if you want to try something really special the following recipe for sirloin stuffed with crabmeat is worth the extra effort.

BROILED VENISON SIRLOIN WITH CRABMEAT

1 backstrap sirloin (about three pounds)
2 cans (6 ounces each) drained crabmeat
    spicy brown mustard

That's all. Either cut a long, lengthwise pocket in the sirloin or poke a deep hole using a carving knife. Raw venison sirloin is particularly tender so be careful not to tear the loin. Stuff the crabmeat deep into this pocket. There's no easy way to do it. A broom handle would work nicely but would be a difficult act to explain if you got caught doing it this way. Work the crabmeat in until the sirloin is plump and full. Coat the sirloin with mustard, just enough to cover the surface. Broil at full flame and turn when the mustard is crusted so the underside can also be coated. The whole cooking process will be finished in just a few minutes, with the length of time depending on the size of the loin, closeness to the flame, and your preference for doneness. A stuffed raw sirloin can also be rolled and tied into a roast.

Venison Roasts

There are two basically different means by which venison or any other meat can be roasted. One method is simple dry roasting, in which the meat (usually a rolled roast) is placed in an oven pan and cooked. Basting or certain other protective coatings might be applied, but a "roasted" roast is cooked chiefly in its own juices. The other method is "braising," which involves the additions of barbecue sauces or other liquids. A braised roast does not need to be rolled, and it can be cooked for a much longer period of time because of the moistening effects of the added juices. The tougher cuts of venison such as the neck and shoulder roasts will be more tender if they are braised.

The rolling of a venison roast for roasting is described in detail in chapter 7. All you do is roll up a large slab of venison and then tie it into a ball with heavy string. The venison round meat (from the haunches) can be butchered into large rounded chunks that don't require rolling. Once a rolled roast has been cooked, the meat will hold the rolled shape when the string is removed for slicing and serving. If you so desire, pieces of beef suet or pork fat can be tucked under the string to provide self-basting during roasting and to add to the formation of gravy juices. If these pieces of domestic fat are tucked deep within the folds of a rolled roast, they usually won't get a chance to melt unless the meat is braised rather than roasted.

VENISON ROAST IN A MUSTARD SHELL

I credit my father with this one. I don't know where he came up with the idea, but I do know that a venison round, sirloin, or rump roast cooked in a mustard shell is something worth remembering. Although it might not strike your reader's palate as being a suitable combination, venison and mustard go together like many other things besides fish 'n chips and love 'n marriage. A rolled venison roast, while still raw, is first smeared with mustard and then placed in the

Fig. 53. A rolled venison roast is most tasty and juicy when served hot and rare.

oven at 350°F. You need not baste this roast nor do you have to prepare for making a gravy. There won't be any juices to speak of because the mustard shell will harden to seal in the natural moistures. After about thirty to forty-five minutes, remove the venison roast from the oven and check it for doneness, cutting deeply to be certain. Don't take any chances. Before the center of the roast is cooked totally to your preference, remove from the heat and let it finish cooking from the heat it has already stored. You will discover that the more subtle shades of mustard flavor will have penetrated into the roast, enhancing the natural taste of venison without having changed it into something else. Leftovers can be thinly sliced into sandwich meat, but there probably won't be any — leftovers, that is.

BRAISED BARBECUE VENISON ROAST

This one is a favorite at our house. The rich, dark red barbecue sauce blends well with the flavor of venison and also has somewhat of a marinating effect on the tenderness of the meat. Venison neck and shoulder roasts are particularly compatible with braising. Mashed potatoes go well with the recipe because the sauce thickens during cooking and provides an excellent gravy with no extra effort required on the part of the cook.

> *1 neck or shoulder roast*
> *3 tablespoons cooking oil (rendered suet can be substituted)*
> *1 stalk celery, chopped*
> *1 clove garlic, chopped*
> *3 tablespoons catsup*
> *6 tablespoons vinegar*
> *3 tablespoons Worcestershire sauce*
> *salt and pepper to taste*

Place the roast in a cooking pan along with the oil, garlic, and celery. Combine the catsup, vinegar, Worcestershire sauce, salt, and pepper in a one cup measure and then add enough water to make one full cup. Pour this tasty sauce over the roast. Cover the pot and cook at 300°F. for about three hours. Check occasionally; add more water as necessary to replenish what is lost to evaporation. If desired, a thin paste of flour and water can be added to the sauce (after the roast is removed) to stretch the gravy.

VENISON BEER CARBONADO

A carbonado is another fine means of preparing the venison neck and shoulder roasts in such a fashion that the meat can be tenderized during a long cooking time. Of course, the venison round and sirloin cuts can also be used, but these choicer cuts are best reserved for grilling or broiling. In a carbonado, the venison is cut into smaller chunks, not bite-sized, but small enough to be easily turned with a fork during cooking. Use a Dutch oven or a covered electric frying pan so that a low, steady heat can be maintained.

> *3 pounds venison neck or shoulder, cut into chunks*
> *2 tablespoons butter or margarine*
> *6 medium onions, chopped*
> *½ teaspoon flour*
> *1 teaspoon sugar*
> *¼ cup consomme*
> *1 cup beer*
> *½ teaspoon salt*
> *¼ teaspoon pepper*
> *1 bay leaf*

Cooking the carbonado involves several steps. First, melt the butter and brown the meat chunks. Then remove the meat. Add the onions and brown. Stir in the flour and sugar and again cook until browned. Finally, add the consomme and beer. Bring to a boil and return the venison to the pan along with salt, pepper, and a bay leaf. Cover and simmer for three hours.

Preparing Venison Stew Meats

Venison stew meat recipes range from the very basic and simple on up through elaborate to highly complex, but they all taste good. Traditionally, the venison stew meats come from the deer's shank and flank meat, which must be cut across the grain into short lengths to partially offset some of the toughness. Many hunters also include the neck and shoulder venison with the stew meat. Of course, any miscellaneous scraps of meat from the rest of the deer, pieces which don't quite make the grade as steaks because of ragged cutting or odd size, can make a valuable contribution to the stew meat stockpile. The tallow is, of course, discarded.

Now let's consider another opinion on stew meat put forth by David Savko, who has worked professionally in the culinary arts and is an expert on venison cookery. Dave maintains that a truly excellent venison stew can only be made with the choicer cuts of venison. He certainly has a point. If one's personal preferences are inclined towards first-class stews as a major means of reducing the size of a venison stockpile, then the better cuts of round and sirloin are best reserved for such use. In that case, the so-called shank and flank stew meat might better be relegated to burger or sausage. The one other improvement that Dave makes to virtually any venison stew involves the addition of red wine. Burgundy is a favorite, but even a very cheap wine (according to Dave, who has tried many varieties) will greatly enhance the more subtle flavors of a stew. You don't taste the wine itself, unless too much has been added. About a third of a cup of wine to two pounds of venison is a good rule of thumb for using wine.

Canned stew meat has the advantage of already being cooked, which saves considerable time during the preparation of a stew, a Stroganoff, or whatever. However, if the tougher cuts of venison have been used for canning, you might see fit to cook the meat a little longer. My wife occasionally prepares hot venison and gravy sandwiches by using canned venison straight out of the jar, and we frankly have no complaints about meat toughness. If toughness can be likened to character, let's just say that these hot sandwiches can be trusted to be a good hearty meal.

HOT VENISON SANDWICH

1 quart canned venison, cubed small
1 6-ounce can commercial gravy
salt and ground peppercorns

Heat and serve on bread or mashed potatoes. That's all there is to it. With a serving of tender string beans, this becomes a complete meal.

Another easy means of preparing venison stew meats is provided by the use of a crockpot cooker. These ceramic cookers are wired to produce a low temperature heat source around the sides of the container rather than on the bottom, and consequently the ingredients to any crockpot recipe can be cooked for very long times without burning or excessive drying occurring. Crockpot cooking is particularly compatible with the tougher cuts of venison because long, moist cooking has a favorable and tenderizing effect on meats. Even whole venison roasts can be cooked in a crockpot. But the crockpot cooking technique works to best advantage in the preparation of venison stews. Meat and vegetables can be tossed into the pot in the early morning, and then after the switch is turned to low heat you can forget about the stew until it's time to serve supper. Both canned and raw venison can be used with equal success in crockpot stew. Raw meat does not require browning before being added.

CROCKPOT VENISON STEW

4 carrots, sliced
4 potatoes, cubed
2 pounds venison stew meat, cubed
1 cup consomme
1 small chunk of beef suet (optional)
salt, pepper, onion powder
1 stalk celery, cut

These ingredients should be placed in the crockpot in the order given above so that the carrots are on the bottom. Cover the pot and set the heat controls according to the instructions with your crockpot. Usually this will be the low setting for nine to twelve hours or the high setting for five to seven hours. During the last half hour of cooking, a small can of peas can be added. A quarter-cup of red wine wouldn't do any harm, either. This crockpot recipe can also be used without a crockpot; just simmer all ingredients except the vegetables in a pan for about two hours. Then add the vegetables and simmer for another half hour.

Venison stew meat also makes an excellent addition to vegetable-based soups if the meat is cubed to extra small sizes. There often is not much difference between a stew and a hearty soup, but if we go by the definition that soup is something that you eat with a spoon, then we can call this next recipe a soup. Of course, how you slurp this one up is your business.

VENISON BEER SOUP

1 *tablespoon vegetable shortening*
2 *pounds venison stew meat, cubed extra small*
1 *pound can tomatoes, cut up*
1 *can of beer*
½ *cup chopped onion*
2 *beef bouillon cubes*
1 *teaspoon brown sugar*
¼ *teaspoon ground peppercorns*
½ *teaspoon thyme*
2 *cups cubed or sliced vegetables*
   (peas, corn, potatoes, carrots, etc.)

Brown the venison in the shortening. Add all ingredients except the vegetables and simmer for about two hours or until the meat is tender. Then add the vegetables and simmer for another half hour. Each preparation of this recipe will provide different flavors depending on which mix of vegetables are used. For a greater shift in flavors, consider including crushed bacon chips and one-eighth teaspoon red pepper. This is your soup now.

Alternate Venison Cooking Techniques

Beyond steaks, roasts, stews and soups, there exists yet another dimension of venison cookery, one which contains the recipes upon which grand reputations as wild game chefs can be built. We might elect to use conventional cooking utensils, the simple tools of campfire cooking, or the space-age technologies of the microwave oven. Regardless of the types of equipment that are employed, an elaborate concoction of venison is successful only if timing and technique have been correct. We pass now into the realm of the experts. But for a while yet, we will still cling to the trusty familiar frying pan.

Venison Burgundy can easily be prepared in less than half an hour from start to finish, but you have to stay close to it all the way. Any tender cut of venison can be used, including the round, the sirloins, the rump, and even the upper shoulder chuck. However, the following recipe by David Savko (of rural New York State—whitetail country!) is proportioned for the two small venison tenderloins. The tenderloins are located alongside the lower spine where they can easily be removed through the abdominal cavity even before the deer is skinned. This means that a celebration dinner of venison can be enjoyed in style on the same day that a whitetail buck gets tagged with your name. You might be tired, washed-out, and excited, but hunger must also be properly accommodated. Here's how to take care of it.

VENISON BURGUNDY

2 *venison tenderloins (approx. 1½ pounds)*
¼ *cup chopped onions*
1 *cup fresh sliced mushrooms*
1 *small minced garlic clove*
⅛ *teaspoon ground ginger*
¼ *cup Burgundy wine*
2 *tablespoons flour*
6 *tablespoons light cooking oil*
   a dash of Worcestershire sauce
   salt and pepper

Slice the tenderloins across the grain into quarter-inch pieces. Place the venison and cooking oil in a small frying pan over a hot fire and brown. When about half-browned, add the onions, garlic, ginger, salt, and pepper. Stir constantly for three or four minutes. Lift the pan from the fire and push the ingredients to one side of the pan. Tip slightly so that the juices drain to the opposite side of the pan. Stir the flour into these juices to make a paste. Return the pan to the fire. Add the wine and Worcestershire sauce and cook for about two minutes more. Serve over hot buttered noodles.

VENISON STROGANOFF

Although the choicest of venison tenderloin and sirloin cuts are preferred for many of the more elaborate venison main dishes, venison Stroganoff can ably handle the somewhat less tender venison round and shoulder meats. This is because the last step of Stroganoff preparations permits a lengthy period for simmering in a skillet. About 1½ hours is usually adequate. At our house, we have often substituted a crockpot for a skillet in that last step, using the low heat setting to achieve a toothsome, tender Stroganoff after six to eight hours of slow cooking.

    2 pounds venison round or shoulder
    4 tablespoons margarine
    ½ pound raw mushrooms
    1 medium onion, diced
 1½ cups beef broth (bouillon)
    1 8-ounce can tomato paste
    2 tablespoons Worcestershire sauce
    1 tablespoon soy sauce
    6 tablespoons flour
    1 cup sour cream
    4 cups hot cooked noodles

Cut the venison across the grain into half-inch slices and then from these cut small short strips. (You can use previously sliced round steaks from the freezer.) Brown these strips in some of the margarine then remove the meat from the fry pan and set aside. Then add to the fry pan the mushrooms, onions, and the rest of the margarine. Cook until onions are tender. Remove the contents and place aside with the venison. Again to the fry pan, add the flour, beef broth, tomato paste, Worcestershire sauce and soy sauce. Simmer for fifteen minutes. Now return to the pan the venison and the other reserved ingredients and cook until the meat is tender. Add the sour cream just before serving and heat through thoroughly. Serve over hot buttered noodles.

STIR-FRIED VENISON WITH CELERY
(David Savko)

This is a venison version of a Chinese dish and is served with cooked rice. Stir-fried venison is a complete meal.

1 pound venison sirloin
4 stalks celery
1 large carrot
1 tablespoon sherry
1 tablespoon soy sauce
1 teaspoon pepper
1 teaspoon sugar
2 tablespoons cornstarch
4 tablespoons oil
1 can 10½ ounce chicken broth

Cut the venison sirloin across the grain into eighth-inch thick slices and then cut these slices into 1"–1½" strips. Combine sherry, soy sauce, pepper, sugar, and one tablespoon cornstarch. Add venison and let stand ten minutes. Meanwhile slice the carrot crosswise into one-eighth-inch-thick rounds and cut celery lengthwise in three-quarter inch wide strips. Cut these strips into two-inch-long pieces. Heat half the oil in a large frying pan. Add venison and stir fry for two to three minutes. Remove venison but keep pan warm. Add the remaining oil and add carrots and celery and stir fry two to three minutes. Mix together another one tablespoon cornstarch and chicken broth in small bowl. Add mixture to vegetables and let thicken while stirring. Add venison and let heat through while stirring continuously. Serve over bed of rice.

CHUCK WAGON VENISON BARBECUE SANDWICH
(Marie Roche)

This one comes from about a mile down the road, where good friends live, and it is a true-and-tested venison recipe that can utilize anything from the choicest of cuts on down to the meanest of venison leftovers. The venison is first completely cooked either by frying or charcoaling (or by grace of being leftover from a previous meal) and is then sliced very thin. When warmed in the barbecue sauce described below and served on crusty rolls, Chuck Wagon Venison becomes choice fare regardless of where the venison originated.

> 2 *pounds cooked venison*
> 1 *cup (8 ounces) tomato sauce*
> ½ *cup water*
> ¼ *cup prepared yellow mustard*
> ⅛ *cup cooking oil*
> 3 *tablespoons brown sugar*
> 2 *tablespoons Worcestershire sauce*
> 1 *teaspoon onion salt*
> 8-10 *crusty rolls*

Combine the tomato sauce, water, mustard, oil, brown sugar, Worcestershire sauce and onion salt (in other words, everything except the venison and rolls) in a saucepan and simmer for at least ten minutes. In the meantime, slice the cooked venison as thinly as possible. Add the sliced venison to the simmering sauce to warm and then serve on the rolls.

VENISON PEPPER STEAKS

Not every venison round or sirloin steak can be cut into nicely symmetrical slabs of even thickness. Usually, when the better-appearing steaks have been wrapped for freezing, there will remain a small pile of odd-sized cuts of otherwise tender venison which seem to fall in a classification of their own. Sandy Thayer, wife of one of America's better deer hunters (or, maybe just one of the luckiest), has resolved this problem of what to do with those cuts by preparing them as peppersteak. Here's how she does it:

> 1 *pound venison steak scraps*
> ¼ *cup chopped onion*
> 1 *dash garlic salt*
> 2 *tablespoons cooking oil*
> 1 *cup hot water*
> 1 *teaspoon beef boullion granules*

> 1 medium green pepper, sliced
> 1 pound can tomatoes
> 2 tablespoons cornstarch
> 2 tablespoons soy sauce

Slice the venison into quarter-inch thickness. Cook the venison, onions, and garlic salt in hot oil in a fry pan until the meat is browned. Add water and the beef boullion; cover and simmer until the meat is tender (about one hour). Add the sliced peppers and tomatoes and cook until the peppers are tender. Then blend the cornstarch, soy sauce, and about a quarter-cup of water into the meat mixture, and stir until thick. Serve over rice or noodles.

VENISON MINCEMEAT

And now, it's time for dessert. A saucy mincemeat pie, served warm and perhaps with a scoop of ice cream, is a fine and fitting dessert to serve at the end of a wild game supper. It is made with ground venison burger. The following recipe also calls for the addition of beef suet, but if your venison burger is already blended with a domestic fat (and it probably is), then just omit the extra suet and use a full 2½ pounds of burger.

> 2 pounds venison burger
> ½ pound beef suet, ground (unless already in burger)
> 1½ pounds apples, diced small
> 2 pounds raisins
> 1 quart cider or orange juice
> ½ tablespoon ginger
> ½ tablespoon ground cloves
> ½ tablespoon nutmeg
> ½ tablespoon cinnamon
> ½ teaspoon allspice
> ½ tablespoon salt
> 1 pound brown sugar

Combine all the above ingredients in a large pot. Break the venison burger apart and stir to get a good mix. Simmer the whole sweet-smelling mass for two hours with the pot covered. Stir occasionally to prevent clumping. The cooked mincemeat can then be used immediately for pies or can be frozen. For pie baking, combine two pounds of mincemeat with one cup of fresh, chopped apples.

Campfire Shortcuts

Some of the world's best meals have been prepared over a campfire, that's for certain. There is something very special, almost intangible, about the aromas that waft from the campfire at mealtime. Some of these qualities are derived from the hardwood smoke. In fact, meats cooked over an open flame are often partially smoked even if a cloud of smoke is not visible. That's because the superheated column of air rising from a wood fire contains combustion products such as phenols, ketones, and aldehydes which help flavor cooked meats and other campfire preparations. Of course, we don't really want to know all this. We would prefer to believe that the very special flavors of campfire foods are caused by the magical properties of sunrises or starlight or something like that.

The smoked flavor of campfire steaks or roasts can be enhanced if the venison is first hung by the fire for a couple of hours or more, positioned so that the meat is touched by the smoke but not the heat. A smoldering, lazy campfire with a minimum of open flame works best for this. Use hardwoods only; the evergreens contain resins which cause a bitter taste. You might want to build a smoking rack from green saplings, around which can be draped plastic sheeting (or your partner's poncho) to confine the smoke.

Virtually all the fry pan recipes described in this chapter, from simple pan-fried steaks to the more complicated stir-fried venison with celery, can be prepared over a campfire. That's obvious; heat is heat, and the temperature of a glowing bed of hot coals can be carefully controlled almost as closely as with a modern stove. Even whole roasts can be successfully cooked if you have the right kind of pot. But oftentimes, the secret to the best campfire meals rests with the magic of sheer simplicity, with a little help from aluminum foil and just a few condiments. A very tasty meal of venison, potatoes, and cooked vegetables can be made with the slightest of effort by wrapping all the ingredients in two or more layers of aluminum foil and then by burying this package in the hot coals of the campfire. That's all there is to it. You don't even have to worry about leaving the foiled meal in the coals too long. Here's the reason: Because the tightly sealed aluminum foil prevents the escape of the natural moistures of the contents, the internal temperature of the package is kept below the range of burning temperatures. The meat and vegetables are literally steamed in their own juices, an action that both tenderizes and improves the flavor of your meal. Wood embers glow at about 450°–500°F., which is really not a great deal hotter than the high setting on a modern oven range. Just be careful that the campfire doesn't break out into open flame.

The venison tenderloins are the most accessible cuts from a deer that is not yet skinned or butchered, but a goodly size portion of round steak can easily be obtained by peeling the hide from around an upper rear leg. (I'm assuming that your campfire cooking will take place at deer camp, where at least one hunter is happy.) Cut the venison into one-inch cubes and season with salt and pepper. Place these on a sheet of sturdy aluminum foil along with sliced potatoes, onions, carrots, peas, and any other raw vegetable that happens to be handy. Spices can be added and will be more effective if rubbed directly on the surfaces of the venison. Lift two opposing ends of the foil and then crimp them tightly together as though you were closing a paper bag. Close the other two ends of the package, but not too tightly. You want the foil to be airtight, but some space underneath should be left so that steaming actions can take place. A second layer of aluminum foil should then be wrapped around the first and it also should be crimped to be airtight. Even a tiny hole can permit enough vapor to escape during cooking that the contents would dry out and then burn. As long as the foil remains airtight, the package can be left in the coals. Half an hour is generally sufficient cooking time for about a pound of vittles, but a longer time will additionally tenderize both the vegetables and the venison.

Variety Venison Meats

There are between three and five pounds of venison on a whitetail deer that many folks will not even acknowledge the existence thereof, let alone discuss the merits of cooking and eating. I'm talking about

Fig. 54. The liver (left) and heart (right) are two venison organs that can provide several delicious meals if properly prepared. These are removed from the carcass during field dressing.

the liver, the heart, the tongue, and the brain. These deer organs are simply no more and no less than pure 100% venison, and any bias against using them as foods is usually based more upon their source and function than on their flavors. In that regard, I would then ask those biased individuals to ponder the source and function of a chicken's egg. Actually, the venison variety meats provide tasty and interesting table fare, and anyone having even the slightest inclination towards claiming status as a wild game gourmet should try the following recipes at least once. The odds are good that these culinary adventurers will never again discard the variety meats.

Venison liver, for example, is surprisingly tender and tasty when it has been properly treated and chilled as soon as possible after the kill. This point cannot be stressed too greatly. A fresh venison liver should be dunked in cold water so that it can rapidly cool, thus preserving the delicate flavors. If this is not possible, the fresh liver should at least be placed in a cool area until it can be given better care. This is not to say that a venison liver that has spent half a day in the trunk of a car won't be any *good*. No, we're saying that a quick chill and soaking is what's necessary to make it *great*.

LIVER AND BACON

For an excellent liver-and-bacon meal, slice about a pound of venison liver into half-inch thick pieces. In a large fry pan, fry a dozen strips of bacon. Pour off part of the grease and remove the bacon to drain. Dip the liver in flour and then plunk these morsels into the hot fry pan. The three secrets of cooking venison liver are to do it fast, do it fast, and do it fast. The longer you cook it, the tougher it will get. We usually fry an amount that can be eaten within a short time and keep the fry pan going on our second and third batches. By not cooking all the liver at once, we are able to maintain a steady flow of hot, tender liver from stove to tabletop and not let our supper get a chance to get cold. Anyone who cooks liver so long that it curls up at the edges is a culinary masochist.

LIVER AND GREEN PEPPERS

For those folks who prefer their venison liver to be cooked well-done, this liver and peppers recipe is the solution to the toughness problem. Possibly, the high acid content of the green peppers has a marinating effect on the liver when these two ingredients are cooked together. Bill Sheesley, a country neighbor and fellow deer hunter, starts out by slicing a couple of green peppers into a fry pan along with some bits of onion. These are cooked until tender. Some, but not all, of the watery fluid that forms is decanted. The strips of liver are then dipped in flour and from there are slopped in with the green peppers. Bill's preference is to cook equal amounts of liver and peppers together, and he keeps the pan on the fire until the liver is cooked all the way through, and maybe even a little longer than that. I have partaken of this simple concoction and was pleasantly surprised to discover that the liver was nicely tender, with a mild peppery flavor.

A venison heart is a remarkably solid chunk of meat. There are two thumb-sized hollows (the ventricles), but the rest of the heart is fine grained muscle that has an interesting texture and good flavor. I usually pickle the heart (see chapter 8), but we have also enjoyed braised venison heart filled with spicy stuffing. Before cooking the heart, first remove the white tallow that usually covers the top end and then peel off the transparent membrane that surrounds the entire organ. For most venison heart dishes, the heart should first be boiled for two to three hours. However, in the following recipe for stuffed heart, the long period of braising serves this same purpose.

STUFFED VENISON HEART

1 venison heart (about one pound)
1 cup herb-seasoned bread crumbs
½ cup diced apple, celery, and onion
1 10-ounce can beef consomme
¼ cup water

Blend the apple, celery, and onion with the seasoned bread crumbs. Add water to moisten. Cut the heart down one side to open and pack the stuffing into it. Fasten partly shut with skewers or simply tie with string. Place heart in a Dutch oven; add consomme and water. Cover tightly. Simmer on top of range or in 325°F. oven for two hours or until tender. Slice to serve.

Venison tongue is larger than many hunters realize because most of it remains out of sight during normal butchering. The tongue is plumply rounded along a greater share of its length, resembling what we think of as a "tongue" only at the outer tip. There is enough good venison in a tongue to provide servings for two, especially if combined with something like buttered spinach or Harvard beets. The flesh is tender when adequately cooked. Tongue can also be served cold as a sandwich-type meat or pickled as described in chapter 8.

The following recipe provides a means of serving venison tongue in truly spectacular style.

Fig. 55. A stuffed venison heart is a very appropriate celebration dinner and a very tasty morsel.

GLAZED VENISON TONGUE

1 venison tongue (obviously)
½ cup crushed pineapple
1 tablespoon brown sugar
1 teaspoon grated orange peel

Boil the tongue for two hours then plunge tongue in cold water. Skin on the tongue will have whitened and can now be easily peeled away. Place tongue in a small baking dish. Prepare the glaze by mixing the pineapple, brown sugar, and orange peel. Spread over the tongue. Cover. Cook for half an hour in 350°F. oven.

(Note: to change the shape and appearance of this somewhat unusual exotic, roll the tongue up into a ball and secure with string.

When originally boiled in this position, the tongue will hold that same shape during the glazing step.

Venison brains can be served in a sauce with other venison dishes, as a unique party snack ("What *are* these delicious little morsels?"), or even simply fried or scrambled with eggs. In many countries of the world, notably France, cooked brains are considered to be a delicacy. We perhaps owe it to ourselves to discover whether or not we've been missing out on a good thing. Venison brains can be easily removed from the deer when the antler skull cap is sawed free. Raw brains are soft and very tender and need to be precooked in order to be firm enough for additional preparations.

VENISON BRAINS

To precook, heat a pan of water to boiling. Add the brains and a teaspoon of lemon juice. Cover and simmer for fifteen minutes. Then plunge into cold water. Peel off the thin membrane that encases the brain.

Now the venison brains are ready to be braised, creamed, broiled or fried. To fry, cut into half-inch slices and dip into a slightly beaten egg. Then coat with crumbs or flour. Fry in margarine until golden brown.

Chapter 10

Tanning Hides

The Value of Deerhides

Let's not even discuss whether or not a deerhide should be thrown away with the bones. The skin of a whitetail deer has a very real commercial value and to waste such a commodity would be outright nonsense. This situation leaves us with three options. We can (1) sell the deerhide while it is still raw, or (2) have the hide tanned professionally, or (3) do the tanning ourselves. Obviously, a decision is needed here, so let's talk about it some more.

Several hundred thousand raw deerhides are sold each year, usually to taxidermists and fur buyers who then turn around and sell them in bulk to the leather industries. There, along with the hides of domestic animals, deerhide is fashioned into a wide assortment of leather goods which ultimately are sold back to us, the consuming public. The odds are good that many of these items are purchased by anti-hunters who, if informed that their favorite wallets, purses, or gloves were very possibly made from genuine deerhide, might for at least one brief moment be able to grasp the concept that the wild whitetail deer is truly a usable natural resource.

The value of a raw deerhide fluctuates right along with the overall hide market. For a few years up until 1982, deer hunters received about six to eight dollars for a raw skin in good condition. However, by late that same year, certain shifts in the market caused the price to drop sharply. Many taxidermists and other buyers barely broke even at two and three dollars a skin but continued to purchase hides with hopes that the market would rise again. During this same time, the price of tanned leather did not change very much at all, at least not in comparison to raw hides. Tanned deerhides were worth twenty to forty dollars, sometimes more. That's because the value of a tanned hide incorporates the costs of tanning, so the supply of tanned hides was adjusted to fit the demand.

If you're wondering what all this has to do with you and your deerhide, consider the fact that, although the value of raw deerhide might fluctuate wildly from year to year, a tanned deerhide will more than likely remain fairly stable in value. Even if you presently have no real interest in leathercraft or have no hot desire to wear deerskin apparel, consider the possibility that someday you might experience a change of mind. Or, maybe someone else in the family will get the urge to do beautiful things with deerhide. Even in its uncut form, whether the hair has been removed or left in place, a tanned deerhide has a certain intrinsic value as a hunter's trophy. Many hunters routinely arrange to tan, or pay to get tanned, every deerhide that comes into their possession.

Whether to Do Your Own Tanning

Yes, it is possible to have too many hobbies. The veteran do-it-yourselfer is often so busy at such a wide variety of self-imposed tasks that the pleasures of achievement get diluted. For what it's worth, I don't really care whether you do your own tanning or pay someone else to do it. But before you squirm completely off the hook of another new endeavor, let's take a look at some of the advantages of home tanning.

Much of the physical work of factory tanning is accomplished by special machines, and those machines are good at what they do — maybe even too good. A factory-tanned deerhide is often so perfectly scraped, sanded, and softened that it resembles a rather handsome

Fig. 56. A tanned deerhide ought to look like a deerhide. This vest, worn by Howard Roche, certainly fits the bill.

piece of synthetic vinyl. ("Oh . . . is that really leather?") Leather tanned at home will usually have a comparatively rough texture on the flesh side and will show certain interesting little imperfections on the grained (hair) side. Generally, if you're going to wear leather, you want it to look like leather. In particular, muzzle-loaders and other outdoor adventurers who have incorporated the costumes of the frontiersmen into their organized shooting competitions prefer that their apparel look like the real thing. That preference alone is often sufficient to justify home tanning.

Another justification to do your own tanning can be found in the cost to have that same job done commercially. An average size deer-hide generally costs between twenty and thirty dollars for factory tanning. Sometimes you can get it done for less than that if you are able to locate a leathercrafter who tans his own hides in a small-time operation. Near where I live along the Pennsylvania–New York State border, there are Amish people who make most of their own goods, and it is usually possible to get deerhides tanned at a reduced price by one of these gentle folks. The cost for mail-order chemicals to do your own home tanning usually runs about five dollars for enough material to tan two or more deerhides. As far as equipment is concerned, tools adequate for getting the job done can be rigged from normal kitchen or tool bench utensils.

One other benefit of doing the tanning yourself is that the ragged edges of the hide will not be excessively trimmed. Usually this is not important. Factory-tanned hides are trimmed so that they will be more symmetrical and less awkward for machine processing. Long lengths of hide from the legs are also cut away for that same reason. These regions that end up missing from the tanned hide are usually not worth anything for leathercrafting. However, for the hunter who wants to use a tanned hide as a form of trophy (perhaps tacked on a den wall), the roughly rectangular shape of a commercially trimmed hide could be a real disappointment because it would not truly resemble an animal hide. If you want the traditional outline of a deerhide, which would include the neck and upper legs, then you had better shy away from factory tanning. The most certain fact about home tanning is this: the hide you start out with is still the same one when you're finished. Hides to be factory-tanned are usually identified by the taxidermist or other middleperson with a coded series of punctures near the edge of the hide. Assuming that the factory ships the right bundle of tanned hides back to the right taxidermist, and assuming that the taxidermist kept good records or at least didn't leave the front door open during a windstorm, the right deerhide will return to you, bullet holes and all. The odds are good that this will happen. But, every year, a small percentage of us end up with someone else's deerhide.

How difficult, how big a job is home tanning? Well, it falls somewhere between laying linoleum and scraping the paint off a badly weathered garage. The amount of care and attention you devote to any of these projects will determine the quality of the end result.

Hair or Bare

Be advised that if you arrange to send a deerhide off to be factory-tanned, and you provide no other instructions, the hide will come back to you bare of hair. The hide will be a piece of leather. If you plan to do some leather working, then a bare deerhide is what you want. However, if you had envisioned that the hide would be returned in the form of a luxurious pelt, a mere flap of leather would instead be a disappointment. In order for the hair to be left on the hide, special arrangements need to be made, such as paying roughly fifty percent more money. Tanning with the hair left on is more expensive (unless you do it yourself) for a couple of good reasons. First, because the thick coat of deer hair fills so much space, fewer deerhides can be processed at one time in a factory vat. Secondly, a hair-on hide requires special processing in that it must be omitted from one step in the tanning sequence and inserted instead in a different step. This complication requires extra time and attention. (But not if you do it yourself. In fact, it's *easier* to leave the hair on!)

The cost of getting a deerhide tanned into bare leather is charged at a flat rate per hide, but the hair-left-on fee is calculated on a square footage basis. (Let's not bother to question why.)

A whitetail deerhide tanned with the hair intact is one of hunting's better trophies. Tacked to a wall on a red or green felt backing, a deer pelt is a mighty handsome display for a den or hunting lodge. A deer pelt can be used as a decorative throw rug, a unique comforter, a lap blanket, or whatever. A pair of pelts can be sewn into a warm vest.

Unfortunately, a deer pelt cannot withstand much physical abuse.

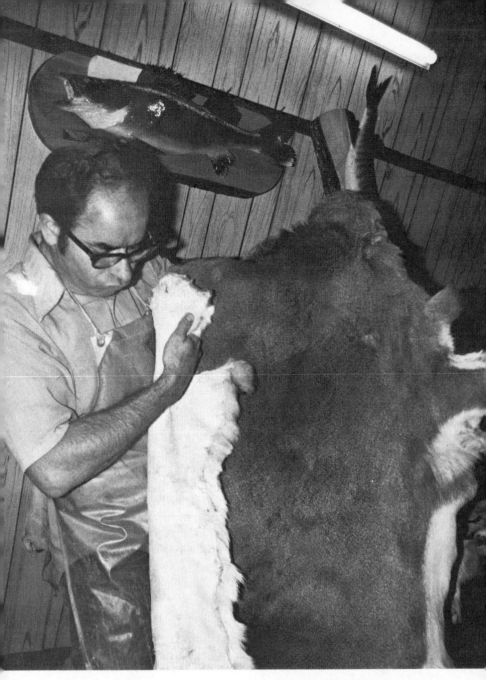

Fig. 57. A tanned deerhide rug with the hair still in place makes an attractive trophy.

A deerhide throw rug should not, for example, be walked upon any more than absolutely necessary. The reason is that deer hair is brittle, and small bits of hair will break free whenever a force is exerted on a pelt. Even when put to use for the more gentle applications, such as a blanket, a certain amount of breakage will occur. This will give the appearance of shedding, but a properly tanned deerhide does not shed; the hair roots remain intact while the outer lengths snap off and fall away. This is a drawback of hair-on deerhide, one that you should seriously consider if a hair-or-bare decision is still pending.

The leathercrafter has no such dilemma; he or she wants that hair removed so that the fabrication of leather goods can begin unhindered.

How to Tan a Deerhide

Home tanning can be made easier if you have all the proper tools and equipment. That's obvious. But don't let a lack of professional devices discourage you from stepping right into this project with confidence. For the tanning of one or two deerhides, which is not that big a deal, you probably have all the equipment you'll need.

Tanning Chemicals

The tanning chemicals are another matter. Some ingredients can be obtained locally, but the easiest route for a small-time home tanning project is to simply purchase tanning agents from an established supplier. One such supplier is the Western Products Company, Mason City, Iowa, 50401, and it is with their kind permission that we are able to describe the actual ingredients of some formulas on the following pages. As an alternative to doing your own mixing of these ingredients, special kits of fully blended powders and compounds that are available by mail order from such companies as Western Products are probably, in the long run, your best bet for lowest cost and least runaround. This way, you don't end up buying more than you really need.

Tools and Equipment

Very few tools are needed for home tanning. A sharp hunting knife, a smooth-edged carving knife, a hatchet blade, and something in the order of a sturdy fencepost, will serve all your needs during the steps of fleshing, oiling, and softening a deerhide. A large container, preferably a clean garbage can, will serve as a soaking and tanning vat.

Tool	Use
Hunting knife	For skinning and the rough trimming of adhered flesh and fat.
Carving knife	A twelve-inch-long, smooth-bladed edge is preferred for use in fleshing the green hide. Insert the tip of the knife in a small block of wood (or wrap the tip in leather) so the knife will have a handle on either end.
Hatchet blade	A dull blade is preferred because no cutting will be done. The hatchet is used during the "slicking" operation to stroke softening oils into the tanned hide.
Post	A fencepost, a carpenter's sawhorse, a porch railing, or virtually any sturdy (but narrow) structure can be used as a support during fleshing and for later breaking up and softening of the leather.
Container	A plastic garbage can is just the right size and substance for holding the pickling and tanning solutions. If not available, use stainless steel, glass, stoneware, a wood barrel, or an enameled container. (Bare iron or aluminum will react with the tanning solutions and ruin their effectiveness.)

Do your tanning where the temperature will remain fairly constant around 70°F. If too cool, the chemicals won't always be as effective, and if too warm, the hide might spoil in between soaking stages.

Salting and Fleshing

Soon after a deerhide has been skinned from the carcass, all the adhered chunks of fatty tallow and bits of flesh should be cut away. (It has been my personal experience that a couple of barn cats can very nicely and neatly attain this same objective within just a few hours of leisurely dining.) Then the bare side of the hide can be salted with uniodized salt, using about one pound per five pounds of hide. Rub the salt into every square inch of hide and then fold the hide over onto itself (flesh side in) and roll this "sandwich" up into a ball. Deerhides are temporarily preserved by salting and can be kept for three to five months at moderate temperatures without spoiling. They also remain reasonably pliable.

However, only a few days of salted storage are necessary for this first step of the tanning sequence. Salting softens the slick membrane

Fig. 58. Fleshing removes the slick membrane on the flesh side of the hide, resulting in a more supple leather.

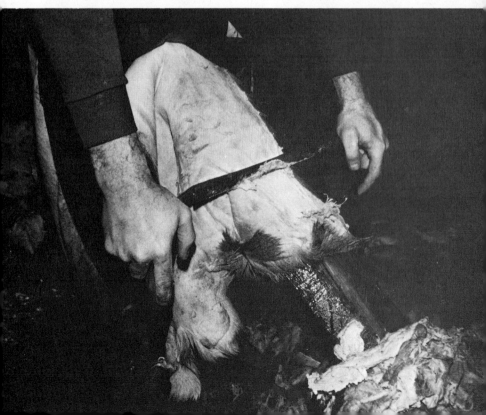

that covers the flesh side of the hide and permits this tissue to be removed more easily during fleshing. Fleshing is essentially a scraping action; we could just as well use an old skate blade instead of the carving knife that we have modified into a fleshing tool.

If the hide had been allowed earlier to dry as stiff as a sheet of cardboard before salting and fleshing could be done, it must first be soaked in water until pliable. For a soaking that will last more than a few hours, add a quarter-pound of borax to the water to prevent spoilage. Then wipe dry and later salt the hide as described above.

Now place the salted hide, bare side up, over your fencepost or carpenter's sawhorse or similar rig and thoroughly flesh it until all of the membrane and other loose tissues have been removed. Don't dig deeply into the hide but instead work at it with a scraping motion, much in the same way you would remove chewing gum from the bottom of a shoe. This step of tanning is probably the most time consuming. When finished with fleshing, wash the deerhide in clear water to dissolve any remaining salt. Use the hatchet blade, if you wish, to slick away the rinse water.

Removing the Hair

If you prefer to leave the deer hair on the hide, skip this step and proceed to "pickling." Otherwise, proceed as follows.

Each hair root is held in place by a bit of fatty tissue. This tissue can be weakened and then destroyed by soaking the hide in a lime solution. This is prepared by mixing about a pint of hydrated lime (builder's lime) to each gallon of water. Or, you can use the same amount of hardwood ashes in addition to the lime and get better, quicker results. If you can't locate a source of lime, use a gallon of ashes to a gallon of water. Within a few days of soaking, the hair will be loosened to the point that all of it can be rubbed off. This messy feat can easily be accomplished by draping the hide over a railing where it can be briskly stroked with a stick or a dull hatchet blade.

After all the hair is removed, the lime must be removed in order that the hide can be tanned. First rinse the hide in cold water; a well-aimed garden hose is fine for this purpose. Then soak the hide for several hours in any *one* of the following solutions:

Fig. 59. Taxidermist Ted Wilson works a hide over a circular saw blade.

    —1 ounce lactic acid to 3 gallons water, *or*
    —1 gallon sharp vinegar to 3 gallons water, *or*
    —¾ pound borax to 3 gallons water.

Finally, rinse the hide one more time to remove any residual solution.

At this point in the tanning operation, if you tack the hide to a vertical surface and permit it to dry, the end result will be a "rawhide" that can be fashioned into lampshades. "Rawhide" will have been adequately preserved by the preceding soaking steps and will need no further treatment. It dries to a translucent, and surprisingly thin and stiff, membrane. In order to convert a deerskin into a soft, pliable leather, we will skip the drying and instead continue to the next step.

Pickling

Pickling serves the purpose of expanding certain tissues within the hide so that the tanning solution can later penetrate the fibers. (Note: If you are using any of the tanning compounds produced by the Western Products Company, such as Western No. 100, No. 200, or No. 300, it is not necessary to pickle the hide because these compounds are blended to pickle and tan all in one step.)

A hide can be pickled with the following solution, but be careful: acid is extremely dangerous and poisonous and should be handled with great care. Always add acid to water, rather than adding water to acid, in order to avoid a violent spattering and bubbling action.

      1¼ liquid ounce sulfuric acid
       3 pounds uniodized salt
       6 gallons water

Place the hide in the pickling solution and stir it a couple times a day. Most deerhides will pickle in a single day, but thick old buck hides might require a tad longer. You can tell for sure if a hide is pickled by looking at the color; a fully pickled hide is bright white rather than mottled blue. Finally, rinse the hide in preparation for tanning.

Fig. 60. Taxidermist Ted Wilson examines three pieces of deerhide all taken from the same deer. From left to right: alum tanned, bark tanned, and cured rawhide.

Tanning

At long last, we arrive at the one step for which all the steps combined are named. Tanning is a process which both preserves the hide and permits the natural fibers to retain their resiliency when oiled and finished. There are essentially three different tanning formulas, each of which produces a different color and consistency to the leather. These are described separately in the following text, showing both the specific ingredients you would need for homemade solutions and the corresponding kits that can be obtained from the Western Products Company.

Remember, you only need to use *one* of the tanning formulas shown below.

(1.) "Alum Tanning" produces a very fine textured leather with a *creamy buckskin color.* This formula is particularly suitable for deerhide and can be purchased in the form of No. 100 Western Tanning Compound. A homemade formula for alum tanning is:

> 1 pound alum
> 2 pounds salt
> (Mixed in enough water to cover the hide.)

Soak the hide in this solution for several days, stirring frequently to insure that all surfaces of the hide come in contact with the solution. There is no magic timetable for tanning; when the alum has thoroughly penetrated, the hide will have lost its raw appearance and the individual leather fibers will be distinctly visible. If an inspection of the hide leaves you uncertain, then let it soak for a day or so longer. What's the rush, right?

Finally, remove the hide from the tanning solution, rinse it, and then place overnight in a solution of a quarter-pound of either borax or bicarbonate of soda in enough water to cover the hide. When later rinsed again and dried, the deerhide will be ready for the final step of oiling and finishing.

(2.) "Chrome Tanning" is the fastest of all the tanning methods, producing a *bluish-green color* that is particularly handsome for gloves, vests and other heavy-use apparel which might otherwise show stains.

To make your own chrome tanning salts, use the following formula:

> 1 pound sodium bichromate
> 1 pound 66% sulfuric acid
> ½ pound 42% glucose
> 1 gallon water

(Note: Use a lead, glass, or epoxy tank and add ingredients only in the order listed. A violent boiling occurs when the glucose is added. Sulfuric acid also is highly dangerous. In place of these ingredients, a premixed kit of No. 200 Western Tanning Compound can be used. It is ready to mix with water and is a far safer alternative.)

A good formula for chrome tanning is as follows:

> 1 pound "chrome tanning salts" (No. 200)
> 2 pounds uniodized salt
> (Mixed in enough water to cover the hide.)

Occasional stirring of the soaking hide is particularly important with chrome tanning because blotchy coloring might otherwise occur. Deerhides usually require three to six days of tanning, longer if the hair has been left on the hide. The extent of tanning can be checked by cutting a thin strip from the edge of the hide; a lighter colored center indicates that more soaking is needed. When the tanning is completed, soak the hide overnight in a neutralizing solution of a quarter-pound of cooking soda to five gallons of water. Finally, rinse and dry before oiling and softening.

(3.) "Vegetable-Bark Tanning" results in a *very dark brown leather* that carries a pleasant, woody aroma. In earlier times, bark tannin was extracted by soaking the bark of oak and certain other trees in hot water. Hides required several months of soaking to achieve a complete tanning. Today, the tanning process can be greatly speeded up by using commercially available spruce extracts. A formula is prepared using the following ingredients.

> 1 pound spruce extracts
> (or No. 300 Western Tanning Compound)
> 2 pounds uniodized salt
> (Mixed in enough water to cover the hide.)

Deerhides can be tanned in this solution in as short a time as three days or as long as twelve days if the hair is still on the hide. As with chrome tanning, a thin strip of hide cut from the edge will reveal the depth of color penetration, which is a measure of the extent of tanning. A few extra days of tanning won't harm the hide, so take your time. After tanning is completed, soak the hide overnight in a solution of a quarter-pound of cooking soda in five gallons of water. Rinse thoroughly before oiling and softening.

(4.) "Combination Tanning" speeds up the vegetable-bark tanning process by opening up the fibers of the hide so that the bark tannin can penetrate more quickly. Simply add a half-pound of alum to the bark solution.

Oiling and Finishing

The tanned deerhide can now be oiled and finished to achieve its maximum softness and pliability. For oiling, use pure neat's-foot oil or Western Tanning Oil. This latter item is an emulsified neat's-foot oil base mixture that is soluble in water. Consequently, the Western product can be used on still-wet leather because the emulsified oil will be absorbed by the fibers as the water evaporates. Ordinary neat's-foot oil should not be applied until the deerhide is reasonably dry.

Oiling is accomplished by "slicking" the oil into the hide using any sort of a small, rounded instrument such as a dull hatchet head, a bent pipe, or a block of hardwood from which the sharp edges have been removed. The oil is applied to the grained (hair) side of the hide by being stroked into the skin with the slicking tool. A kitchen table makes an appropriate working surface. Allow the first coat of oil to penetrate and then add a second coating while the leather is still moist. Then roll the hide up so that drying will require at least two days. If drying occurs too rapidly, the hide will become stiff and unwieldy. The drying process can be slowed by covering the hide with wet cloths.

Before the hide gets a chance to dry completely, work the hide flesh side down over a post or stake. Give the hide a good, vigorous workout, but be careful that you don't scratch or damage the smooth grain (hair) side. The more working that the hide receives at this point while still partially moist, the more pliable and soft it will become.

Finally, when the hide is completely dry, the flesh side can be sanded to achieve a soft, suede-like texture. You can control the coarseness or fineness of that texture in the selection of sandpaper, with fine paper creating a more velvety buff. Staple the hide flesh-

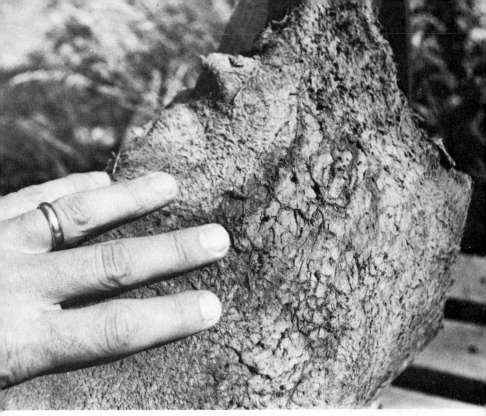

Fig. 61. A close-up of the texture of tanned deerskin that has not been completely finished and sanded. This rough texture is desired for authentic-appearing mountainman apparel.

side up to a flat working surface so the sanding can be done with a minimum of slipping, sliding, and swearing. A carpenter's belt or rotary sander can help you do a more professional job of finishing, with more even results. On the other hand, you might not want to achieve so-called "professional" results with deer leather, particularly if the leather is to be used in the fabrication of authentic-looking mountainman apparel. Certainly a trapper's coat, a black powder bag, and other old-time leather goods will appear more realistic, more reminiscent of the frontier, if the sanding is omitted.

Chapter 11

Whitetail Deer Handicrafts

A Deer Is Not a Kit

There are many other useful and decorative items that a whitetail deer can provide besides venison for the supper table and a mounted head for over the fireplace. Now we're talking about using the tanned leather, the antlers, the hair, and even the tallow as the raw materials for some unique and authentic craft items. Unlike many of the "craft kits" sold today, which require a fair amount of handwork to assemble but which make no demands at all upon your creative intelligence, whitetail handicrafts require both skill and ingenuity. A deer is not a kit; whitetails do not come neatly packaged with pre-punched holes, dotted lines, color-code numbers, and especially a set of instructions folded neatly up inside them. When we make something from the materials provided by a whitetail deer, there is a special satisfaction to be gained from having made a truly genuine article from a natural resource and from having used our own skills and labor to accomplish this goal. In this optimistic and confident frame of mind, we can now look at some of the possibilities contained within the realm of the whitetail handicrafts.

Leathercraft

The necessary techniques for tanning deerhides were described in the preceding chapter. If you, however, choose not to do your own tanning, then that job can be hired out to the professionals — for a fee, of course. Either way, the finished tanned hide will be a surprisingly supple and velvety piece of leather that literally begs to be fabricated into any of a variety of leather goods. The only real limiting factor to those ambitions will be the relatively small size of individual deerhides, which generally run between twelve and fifteen square feet per deer. Sometimes not even all that can be used, particularly if there are several bullet holes marring the otherwise handsome appearance of the hide. In certain leathercraft items, a bullet hole might even add to the "trophy" or interest value. But let's face it; a hole in a glove or a change purse is an obvious defect whether or not there happens to be a story behind it.

Deerhide Color and Thickness: What to Expect

The thickness and color of a tanned deerhide will have much bearing on the type of items that can be made from it. Surprisingly, there is a great deal of variation from one deer to another in the thickness of the skin, although the average is about an eighth of an inch. As might be expected, a yearling deer will have a thinner skin than will a tough old buck. But then, there are often differences even between mature bucks. Until you can hold and touch the finished, tanned hide, you can't be sure whether the hide will be sufficiently thin and pliable for the making of dress gloves, or thick and sturdy enough to be used for moccasins. With a little experience, a guesstimate can be made from the raw skin before it is tanned, but you can't be certain until afterwards. The same degree of uncertainty also applies to color. Some hides naturally take on a darker hue, others a lighter buff color, even when these hides are all tanned together at the same time in the same vat. Then again, the strength of the tanning solution can affect color. You can send two similar hides off to a tanner and later receive two very dissimilar colors. In addition to all this, the three basic tanning formulas (alum, chrome, and bark tannin) each produce distinctly different colors. Alum tanning creates a natural buff to light brown; chrome tanning gives a dark greenish hue, and a bark tannin (hence the word "tanning") formula will produce a very dark brown.

Tanned hides can also be dyed, as long as the original, natural color is light enough to accommodate the new coloring.

The sometimes slight and subtle differences in color and thickness between two deerhides might not seem to be all that important. But if you are trying to match up a pair of hides to make something like a vest or a coat, then you begin to realize the importance of uniformity.

And yes, a vest does require two deerhides. For a jacket, four to six deerhides are needed, depending on the style and size of the jacket and (of course) the sizes of the deerhides. That might not seem possible, but it is true. Partially because of their thick coat of hair, deer appear to be larger and bigger around the middle than they actually

Fig. 62. Two of the author's daughters model deerskin apparel. From left to right, Laura sports an alum-tanned jacket (four deerhides required) and Karin wears a bark-tanned, fringed trapper's jacket (six hides required).

are. Further, a deerhide shrinks during tanning, sometimes up to 20 percent. When the ragged edges of the hide are trimmed, the tanned skin shrinks to an even smaller square footage. In fact, you seldom can get sufficient leather from a single deerhide to make more than three pairs of gloves. Sure, there will be some scraps left over, but these will hardly be worth saving except for possible future repairs to those gloves. Part of the reason that a deerhide produces such a scanty amount of usable leather can be found in the natural symmetry of a hide. The skin is thickest over the region of the spine, tapering slightly towards the edges. The leather for a matched pair of left- and right-handed gloves, for example, should be cut from corresponding left and right regions of the hide. Admittedly, this is not always necessary, but the need is there often enough that variations in thickness and even texture should be checked out carefully before the pattern cutting begins.

Leathercraft Tools and Patterns

Entire books have already been written on the subject of leathercrafting, with "tools and patterns" often requiring a greater share of the total word count. The subject is as extensive as automobile repair, and obviously the type of job that is to be done will determine which tools are needed. Generally, leathercraft items such as gloves or simple vests require no more tools or patterns than can be found in the type of household where socks occasionally get mended, the sort of place inhabited by folks who have the gumption to skin and butcher their own deer. Deer leather is usually relatively thin and pliable, not unlike good chamois, and hence many of the sturdier leatherworking tools are not required. Neither are the mallets, stamps, chisels, punches, and all the other utensils needed for making decorated "tooled" leather items if you have no interest in that particular area of leathercrafting. A punch and a mallet, as well as lacing, will be needed if you desire to lace, rather than sew, the sections of a pattern together. A sturdy pair of shears or a utility knife are all the tools you will need for cutting whitetail deerhide.

For the fancier and more detailed leathercraft items, a complete array of tools and patterns can be obtained via mail order, or directly from various leathercraft or hobby supply stores. Check the classified advertisements in the hunting and fishing magazines for the addresses

Fig. 63. An assortment of leathercraft items made from tanned deerhide. Hides vary in thickness from deer to deer. Thick hides from old bucks are better for moccasins, belts and work gloves.

of those leathercraft companies which are more apt to cater to the peculiar and specialized desires of the outdoor person.

Suggestions for Leathercraft Items

Most of the leathercraft items shown in the following list can be made with a single thickness of deerhide. Certain items such as belts, dog collars, and horse bridles can be made sturdier either by using a second layer or by braiding thongs together. Patterns for all the following are sold by most of the major leathercraft supply houses.

Antler Plaque Covers   Belts
Arrow Quivers   Black Powder Bags
Baby Shoes   Book Covers

Braiding
Carpenter's Aprons
Checkbook Holders
Coasters
Dog Collars
Eyeglass Cases
Gloves
Gun Cases
Handbags
Hunter's Chaps
Jackets
Key Cases
Knife Sheaths
Lacing
Log Carriers
Moccasins
Pistol Holsters
Pouches
Purses
Quirts
Rifle Slings
Sandals
Scabbards
Shirts
Steering Wheel Covers
Thongs
Tobacco Pouches
Trapper's Shirts
Vests
Wallets
Watch Bands
Zipper Gussets

Antler Craft Items

The thought of sawing a beautiful set of antlers into smaller sections is enough to make the trophy hunter within us recoil in horror. Aaagh! But let's face it, many buck deer sport antlers that are either too small to qualify as trophies or else are broken or deformed. Such antlers are prime candidates for being formed into antler buttons, handles for knives and tableware, and other handsome items that become "trophies" in a different sort of way. The boney substance of which antlers consist can be cut and sanded almost as easily as the more dense hardwoods and will respond well to the use of a power bandsaw or jigsaw. As needed, holes can be drilled with a standard electric drill. I once gave a set of antlers to a dental student, who carved them into miniature figurines with a dentist's drill while practicing to take on bigger game—us. The art of scrimshaw could similarly be done upon deer antlers, if only for the sake of the art itself. Ideally, any of the items fashioned from deer antlers should retain the rough, burled texture so that there can be no mistaking their natural origin. The appearance of antler is often copied in plastic, but you still recognize the real thing when you see it.

Fig. 64. Antler-handled tableware can be made from deer antlers, using ordinary woodworking equipment. (Photo by Don Shiner.)

Antler-Handled Tableware

Slender antlers, or the tines, are particularly suited for use as solid handles for forks, spoons, and knives. As is shown in the accompanying photographs, the antler is first cut to the appropriate length for comfortable use as a handle. A tableware utensil is then cut to a length about an inch longer than will be visible when the antler handle and utensil are assembled. Drill a hole one inch deep into one end of the antler section that is big enough to accommodate the sawed end of the utensil. Fill this hole with epoxy glue that has been mixed with the powder that formed when the sawing and drilling was done. Insert the utensil into its new handle and let the epoxy dry. A power sander can be used to finish off any rough edges.

Hunting Knife Handles

Flat slabs of antler can be sawed to cover the handles of hunting knives. This requires a little more machinery and twice as much patience to achieve a good fit, but the resulting product will be handsome. The heavily knurled base of the antler is needed for large knives and it provides a better grip. The handles of most mass-produced knives were attached with rivets, but the recent developments of special epoxies and "miracle glues" has provided a means of attachment that is equal, or even superior to, that provided by rivets. In fact, a good share of today's custom-crafted knives that sell for many dollars are fabricated with the help of epoxies.

Antler Buttons

An antler button is no good at all if it is too big or too small to fit a certain buttonhole, so check this out before you start cutting.

Fig. 65. For antler-handled tableware, antlers must first be cut to an appropriate size for use as handles. (Photo by Don Shiner.)

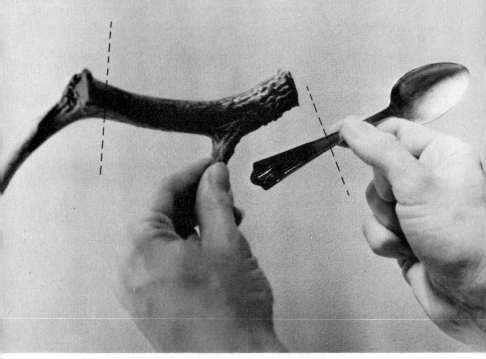

Fig. 66. The utensil also is cut, slightly larger than what will be visible when assembled. A one-inch hole is drilled into the antler and filled with epoxy glue. The utensil is then inserted. (Photo by Don Shiner.)

A power bandsaw works best for sawing antler buttons because a straight, smooth cut is required. Buttons should be about one-eighth inch thick, which doesn't leave much room for error. These antler slices can then be sanded on the outward-facing surface, but there's no need to achieve a perfect polish. In fact, a rough-hewn surface provides a more authentic appearance. Drill holes as needed for sewing; one-sixteenth-inch diameters will accommodate sturdy thread. You might want to bevel the edges of these holes with a touch from a larger drill bit, just enough to keep the thread from later fraying. A coat of varnish or shellac will bring out the natural highlights of antler buttons.

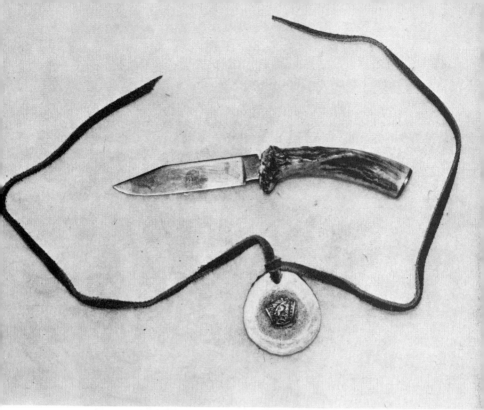

Fig. 67. An antler-handle hunting knife and an antler medallion, both crafted by Jerry Quinn.

An Antler Pipe

A truly unique smoking pipe can be fashioned from the junction of the brow tine and the base of an antler. The tine forms part of the pipestem, while the flared burl (where the antler attaches to the skull) becomes the open bowl of the pipe. Friends of mine spotted such a pipe in western Pennsylvania, but I have not been able to locate the man who carried it to determine whether his pipe smoked cool and sweetly. Let's assume that it did and still does. The bowl had been bored nearly to the bottom, and the tine had similarly been drilled to provide an opening to the bowl. A plastic mouthpiece of the kind that comes with disposable corncob pipes had been fitted to the working end of the pipestem.

Antler Fireplace Tool Rack

Using a relatively large set of antlers, a sturdy and attractive fireplace tool rack can be constructed. I have not yet made one of these, but the following technique described by Larry G. Baesler sounds as though the job would be a fairly easy one. The four steps which follow originally appeared in *Sports Afield* magazine and are shown here in their entirety.

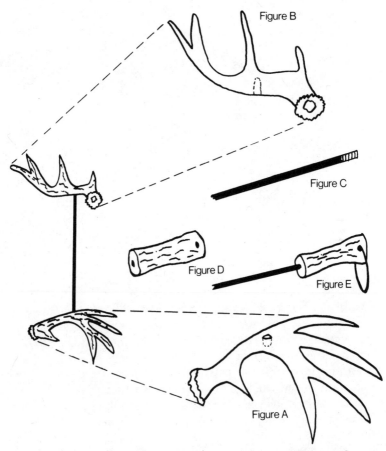

Fig. 68. The steps involved in making your antler fireplace tool rack. See text for instructions. (Courtesy Sports Afield.)

"You will need several items: two antlers removed from the skull plate—they need not be from the same rack; a ⅜″ steel rod approximately 33 inches long, painted to match the color of your fireplace tools; epoxy glue—the quick-set or five-minute variety is preferable; a ⅜″ electric drill and a ⅜″ bit; a small file or hacksaw.

Step 1. Place the antler that is to serve as the base on a hard surface with the points down as in figure 68-A. To get a stable position there must be at least three points touching the surface.

Step 2. Find a point on the top surface of the base antler that is roughly in the center of the contact points. It shouldn't be too far toward either end of the base antler because this will destroy the stability of the finished product. Once you have chosen the center point, drill a ⅜″ vertical hole into the antler as deep as possible without going entirely through it. Put a generous amount of epoxy on the rod tip and into the hole. Now push the rod into the hole as far as possible and let the epoxy set. Make sure that when the base is resting in the normal standing position the steel rod remains vertical.

Step 3. With the points of the antler up as shown in figure 68-B, select a point on the bottom that is approximately in the center. Drill a ⅜″ vertical hole at this point as deep as possible without penetrating the opposite side of the antler. Mount an antler on the rod but do not epoxy into place. Now place your fireplace tools on this hanger antler. Once the tools are in place, rotate the antler on the rod to obtain the position of greatest stability. Once you have determined this position, epoxy the antler into place.

Step 4. (Optional). Fireplace tools with antler handles and leather tongs to hang them by are a nice complement to the rack itself. Remove the handles that are on the tools as shown in figure 68-C. Cut a four- to five-inch section from an antler. Drill a hole in one end for the shaft of the fireplace tool. Make sure that the handle will fit onto the shaft snugly. Now drill a small hole through the other end of the handle section to accommodate a leather thong (see figure 68-D). Epoxy the handle into place, tie a short length of leather thong through the small hole (figure 68-E), and the job is now completed.

Reprinted from Sports Afield *magazine, August 1982 Issue. Copyright 1982. The Hearst Corporation. All rights reserved.*

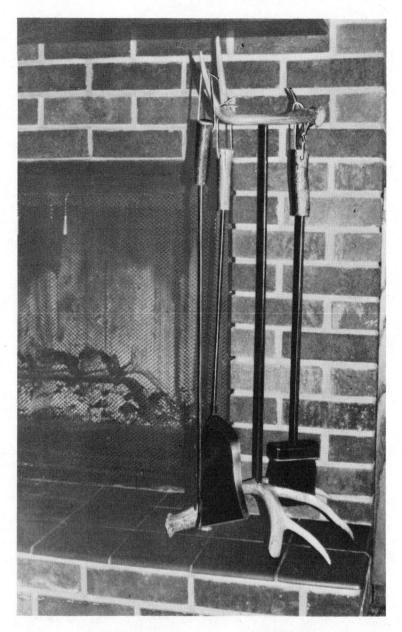

Fig. 69. The completed antler fireplace tool rack.

Deer Hair Fishing Lures

Hunting trophies come in many forms, and deer hair fishing lures made from the coat of a memorable buck qualify for trophy status in very special ways. They bridge the gap between the hunting and angling sports, bringing along luck that often is sorely needed in angling endeavors. Can you sincerely doubt that a "trophy" fishing lure will not attract trophy fish? Of course not! Here's a chance to parlay some of autumn's good fortune into triumphs that come in other forms.

Deer hair possesses some unique properties that make it particularly suitable for the manufacture of a wide variety of artificial fishing lures. The main body hairs on the winter coat of the whitetail deer are essentially hollow; they contain a multitude of tiny air cells which supply the deer with a protective blanket of insulation during the rigors of cold weather. This same feature provides a natural buoyancy in water that most other types of animal hair don't have. The tendency to float rather than sink is a real plus when deer hair is used for dry flies and other surface lures such as bass poppers. The tail hairs, however, don't have these flotation cells (or apparently not as many of them) and can be used instead for underwater lures such as wet flies, jigs, and bucktail streamers. The long tail hairs also have a coarse and crinkly texture which helps prevent matting when the lure is wet so that its action and appearance are not similarly dampened.

Examples of classic deer hair lures include the Muddler Minnow, Mickey Finn, Rat-faced McDougal, the Irresistable, and a variety of round-bodied insect dry flies such as ants, wingdings, houseflies, beetles and bees. Large full-bodied lures made using the spun deer hair method include variations of moths, frogs, mice, and bumblebees. There literally are deer hair lures for every method of angling and for every species of freshwater game fish that will take an artificial lure, from the diminutive bluegill on up to the mighty muskellunge.

Deer hair can be dyed green, black, yellow, or whatever colors are needed to simulate the appearance of small creatures that might fall prey to lurking hungry fish. Several deer hair lures, such as brown mice and Muddlers and simple white bucktail streamers, are made using the original, natural colors. Probably the simplest deer hair lure to make is the bucktail streamer, which usually consists of not

Fig. 70. A deer tail with the hairs intact. Deer hair has unique properties which make it especially suitable for use in fishing lures.

Fig. 71. Classic deer hair lures include spun-hair poppers, mouse "gurglers," Muddler Minnows, flies, and wingdings.

much more than a pinch of tail hair tied onto a weighted hook with nylon thread to imitate the shape of a small minnow. Such a lure can be "improved" with painted eyes and a tinsel-wrapped body, but many a lunker fish has been brought to boat or shore with no more than a hook and some deer hair in its gaping mouth.

The "spun hair" method is used for surface lures to create a bulky mass of protruding hairs on the shank of a hook so that, when trimmed—like you would trim a lawn hedge, a spiney resemblance to a rounded body can be created. Use deer hair removed from the back or sides of a deer so that the lure will have those flotation air cells. Make your mouse or bumblebee or other fat little critter by first placing a pinch of hair laterally across the hook shank, near the bend. Wind a length of nylon thread across the hair and around the shank so that the hair is flared into a circle. Loop the thread around the shank once more, following the original path. Repeat this procedure until enough protruding hairs have been packed around the shank that the eye of the hook has been approached. Then tie off and set the end of the thread with waterproof glue. Now the trimming can begin, which will convert the rather grotesque-looking mass of hair into a neatly compacted body. No connoisseur of tasty mice would quit at this point without adding a short length of leather thong to represent a tail. Moths and bumblebees have feathery wings, of course, and frogs have long bucktail hair legs tied and bent at the joints to give a kicking action when the lure is retrieved in jerks.

By my way of thinking, a perfect trio of North American trophies would be an antlered deer head mount, a respectably sized fish mount, and, in between these two, the deer hair fishing lure that made this combination possible.

How to Make Venison Soap

That's right: *soap,* not soup. Venison tallow can be converted into soap, a nice white soap that has a creamy texture, good cleansing properties, and a natural firmness which permits it to be molded into bars. Soapmaking is a rather simple process, not even as complicated as baking an apple pie. We'll go into the details later, but for now, let's just take a look at the basic steps of soapmaking for the

Fig. 72. A bar of the author's homemade venison soap being put to good use. The soap was made from deer tallow removed during butchering.

sake of introduction. First, tallow is rendered into a grease by cooking it. When the grease has cooled off (but not yet hardened), a lye solution is stirred into the grease. The whole mess turns into soap overnight, with a little glycerine formed as a by-product. That's it. The temperatures have to be controlled to within reasonable ranges, and you might want to take the extra steps of adding fragrances or other modifying ingredients, but basic soapmaking is not at all complicated. You can make as small a quantity as one bar of soap or you can shoot the works and make an entire year's supply. And there is the added incentive of value to consider; the monetary worth of the soap that can be made from the tallow of a fat whitetail deer is roughly equal to the cost of a good hunting knife.

But we don't want to always be looking only at the economic payoffs of the utilization of a whitetail deer. There are other benefits.

For example, venison soap provides deer hunters with a means of remaining washed and clean during the deer season without having to smell like one of the synthetic perfumes that are found in commercial soaps. Deer rely more on their sense of smell than sight or sound to detect danger, and a hunter who has washed that day with a natural, unscented soap has a distinct advantage over one who stinks like a chemical factory. Of course, natural scents such as apple or pine might be desired for their cover-up abilities, and essences of these odors can be added during the soapmaking process using totally natural ingredients.

Nicely wrapped bars of venison soap also make unusual and interesting gifts during the holiday seasons. Following the examples set by modern advertising techniques, you could label such gifts with invented brand names like "Antler Essence" or "Buck Fever." Another possibility is "Rutting Season." But don't just write "Venison Soap" on your personalized label; someone might try to eat it.

Another reason, perhaps the major one, for converting venison tallow into a usable product is that we, as responsible sportsmen, want to minimize the waste of a natural resource. If, in the process of totally utilizing a whitetail deer's flesh, fat, and hide, we discover that we have better used our own creative abilities, then we have achieved something that can't be bought in a store the way soap can be. Nowadays, commercial soaps often are not made from the fats of wild creatures nor even from domestic animals. The major ingredients in many of the soaps you buy today are refined from petroleum.

Step 1: Trimming and Rendering the Tallow

Most of the tallow on a whitetail deer is located between the skin and the carcass. Consequently, the tallow can be easily removed in large slabs during skinning. Large pads of white venison tallow usually exist on the hips and around the upper shoulders, and these can be peeled off with help from the skinning knife. There often is another large mass of tallow located along the lower spine inside the abdominal cavity. The remaining tallow on a deer carcass is scattered between the many muscles, and gathering a sizeable amount of it requires a lot of picky work. However, every handful of tallow is equivalent to a bar of soap, so your extra efforts can be considered worthwhile.

Use fresh tallow only. Tallow that has gone rancid might not form into a solid soap. Also, don't use tallow that has been peeled from a salted hide because the salt can cause a separation to occur while the soap is forming. Remove any of the red meat which might remain attached to the tallow. I don't know for certain whether tallow that has been frozen can later be used for soapmaking, but it seems logical that it could be.

Slice the tallow into small, thin chunks so that it can more easily be rendered into a liquid grease. Rendering is accomplished by frying, whether in a stovetop fry pan or in a campfire cauldron. The odor of fried venison tallow is surprisingly repugnant (which is one reason why it should be removed from edible venison), so you might consider the merits of doing the rendering at a time when the odor of the kitchen is not important, like when you're not expecting company. But rest assured, the odor of venison soap is surprisingly fresh and pleasant. When the lye solution is added to melted tallow, a complex organic chemical reaction takes place which alters the structure of the tallow into that of a different substance, namely, soap. There is one other aspect of this chemical reaction that produces an almost magical result, which is that the final amount of soap will be greater than the original amount of tallow. In fact, there will be one and a half times as much soap! If you start out with six pounds of tallow, you will get nine pounds of soap. This is because the water in the lye solution is joined with the tallow to form soap, even firm bar soap that feels dry to the touch. Remember this when you're trimming the tallow because getting something extra for nothing is always enjoyable to contemplate.

When the tallow has been rendered by melting it into a grease, you can either let it cool and solidify for use at a later date, or you can proceed with soapmaking once the grease has cooled to within the range of 130–140°F. A note of caution: as is described in the next section, lye (and the lye solution) must not be permitted to come in contact with certain materials such as aluminum. Once the lye solution is added to the grease, the lye's potency is greatly diluted. However, don't use an aluminum pan to hold the grease if the same container is to be used for soapmaking. Instead, use iron, steel, or an enameled container for the grease.

The soap recipe in this book is based on *six pounds of tallow.* You can make more or less by adjusting the ingredients proportionally, but the technique remains the same.

Step 2: Preparing the Lye Solution

Household lye is stocked by most supermarkets in the section where the heavy-duty cleaning agents and drain openers are kept. Look for a label that states "100% Lye." Most other commercial drain-openers are *not* suitable for soapmaking because they contain additional chemicals, and sometimes aluminum powders, which would interfere with the soapmaking reactions. You're looking for pure lye crystals (sodium hydroxide). While you are there in the store, take a walk past the meat counter and check some of the current prices-per-pound. This experience will make you appreciate venison all the more. And check the cost for a bar of soap because that will give you additional encouragement to make your own.

Working with household lye is a potentially dangerous endeavor; so is driving a car or handling a deer rifle. By applying common sense and by adhering to the specified safety precautions, we can limit the danger and still achieve our goals. Lye, and the solution that will be made for soapmaking, is a very strong caustic chemical agent that can strip the skin from an innocent hand. If such contact should accidentally occur, immediately wash the affected area with water and then apply boric acid for the eyes or vinegar for the skin. I very strongly advise you to read the label on a container of household lye and to do this before you open the can. Be aware of the following rather nasty properties that lye has.

1. Lye can ruin a garbage disposal unit in a sink drain and can raise havoc with certain septic systems.
2. Lye reacts violently with aluminum, so don't use aluminum containers, and don't pour the stuff into an aluminum sink.
3. Pure lye is in the form of dry crystals which can readily absorb moisture from the air. Consequently, the original container should be kept capped so that the crystals within will remain fresh and fully potent.
4. Lye solutions absolutely must be prepared using *cold* water only. Even then, a lye solution becomes intensely hot of its own accord

when mixed with water, and that heat can crack a ceramic or glass container or melt plastic. Later, the solution will cool.

5. Lye, when mixed with water, also spits and gives off fumes that are objectionable at close range. Be cautious.

6. When mixing the solution, add the lye to the measured amount of water rather than the other way around. This helps limit the heat which develops and reduces spitting and spattering.

7. Don't prepare the lye solution until you are ready to use it.

All right, now we can proceed. Most commercial household lye is sold in twelve-ounce cans, and our recipe for soapmaking is geared to use the whole can to prepare an approximate 20 percent solution.

Make the solution by adding lye to the water, not the other way around. Stir with a wood spoon.

1 12-ounce can lye
2½ pints tap water
To add to six pounds of venison tallow.

Step 3: Mixing the Ingredients to Make Soap

We will use all of the lye solution that we made with one twelve-ounce can of lye crystals and 2½ pints of water to convert six pounds of rendered venison tallow into nine pounds of pearly white bar soap. These proportions, with which I have successfully made venison soap, are recommended by the makers of "Lewis-Red Devil Lye."

The temperature of both the lye solution and the tallow should be controlled as is specified below. A dairy thermometer or equivalent type thermometer that registers within the range of 90°–150°F. will provide the best means of control. However, the temperature requirements are somewhat forgiving of minor errors. (Our pioneer forebearers didn't use thermometers!) You can achieve a fairly accurate temperature guesstimate by placing your hand gingerly along the sides of each container. The tallow container should feel just hot enough to be uncomfortable after a few seconds of contact. The lye solution *container* should feel slightly warmer than the warmth of your own tongue. (Say "Ahhhhhh")

More specifically:

Venison tallow at 130°–140°F.
Lye solution at 100°–105°F.

If the melted tallow is a little too cool, it can be reheated. So can the lye solution, but only with great care since the nasty stuff is so reactive. The lye solution will naturally cool down to the proper temperature as it loses the heat it generated during mixing with water. Ideally, you can keep an eye on the lye temperature while it cools, and then start making soap as soon as the lye and tallow temperatures are each within the proper ranges.

Begin by pouring the lye into the tallow slowly in a thin stream. You want to avoid heavy concentrations of lye, even temporarily. Stir the mixture slowly and evenly while the lye is being added. (It's best to have someone helping you at this point.) Continue stirring after the lye is gone, usually for about fifteen minutes or until the mass begins to turn white and thicken. Too rapid stirring will cause the soap to coagulate and then separate into two different substances.

Then pour the entire contents into a shallow cardboard box that you have lined with plastic wrap. Keep the filled box warm by placing a blanket over it so the soapmaking reaction (it's called "saponification") can continue for a while longer. The stored warmth improves and smooths the texture of the soap. Don't disturb the soap for at least twenty-four hours. The next day, you can remove the virgin soap either by tugging against the plastic wrap or by tearing the cardboard away from your new treasure. (If you have elected to only make a pound or two of venison soap, a glass pie plate can be used instead of the box, but make sure it is about the same temperature as the soap when you do the pouring.)

The soap can now be cut into bars. A knife will break it into chunks, so cut the soap by cinching strong twine or wire around the slab. Pull both ends tight and the soap will cut very neatly. The soap can be used immediately, but it improves greatly with aging. Ideally, the bars should be stored at room temperature for two weeks.

Modifications of Venison Soap

1. A liquid substance called glycerin is also produced during soap-making but usually remains locked within the soap. Sometimes, however, part of the glycerin settles out as a bottom layer underneath the soap. This is more apt to occur if the soap mass was stirred too rapidly, if the temperatures were not quite right, or if salt was present. But that's all right: glycerin can be used as a hand lotion. Glycerin-and-rosewater used to be the standard treatment for ladies' chapped hands. Save this liquid, and you will be the only kid on your block with a venison hand lotion.
2. Venison soap can be converted into the floating variety by whipping the thick saponified mixture just before it is poured into the box. A wire whisk can be used. If the mixture is nicely whitened (indicating that the lye is just about neutralized), a food blender can be used to foam the soap before it hardens.
3. Venison soap can be scented. In olden times, the soap bars were wrapped in blossoms or leaves, but I don't know how effective this procedure was. According to Linda Burton of the Cooperative Extension Service, various commercial oils of clove, cinnamon, lavender, and other herbs can be stirred into the thickening mixture with pleasing results. Such oils can usually be obtained at pharmacies, from candymakers, and through herbal mail-order catalogs. Consider, however, the cost of these oils when making your something-for-nothing venison soap. Incidentally, commercial essences used for cake flavoring and similar applications contain alcohol which can interfere with the formation of soap. There really is no reason to add a scent to venison soap other than to have taken that extra step with your creative abilities. I have made venison soap, and it's my opinion that the natural unmasked odor is just fine the way it is. No, there is nothing "wild" about the odor. If forced to come up with a description, I'd say that venison soap smells like soapy bread.
4. The sudsing action can be improved by adding two tablespoons of borax to the cooling solution of lye. Use less borax if you used

less than the full twelve-ounce can of lye. Borax is essentially the same substance that you would find in a box of laundry Boraxo. By itself, venison soap does not work up much of a lather. In fact, a technical argument *against* excessive lathering could be made because the soap contained in bubbles is being held away from the surface you are trying to clean.

5. Liquid venison soap jelly can be made by slicing one pound of soap into a gallon of water. Boil until dissolved and then store in a closed container. Soap jelly can be used for hand washing; it also can be used for the laundry. I know one person who uses homemade soap jelly on goats' udders. As a hair shampoo, venison soap jelly might not pass the test because it requires much rinsing compared to modern synthetic shampoos.

Other Fats, Other Soaps

Other fats and certain vegetable oils can be blended with venison tallow in combinations that will produce soaps having slightly different textures and qualities. These modified soaps are more effective over a wider range of water temperature in both soft and hard water. The soapmaking technique remains the same; only the temperatures need be changed. Animal fats having high melting and solidifying temperatures are best for soapmaking. This fact places venison tallow at the top of the list as probably the best soapmaker. Ironically, the same trait that flunks venison tallow from cooking school (that is, the fact that it hardens too quickly in cooked venison) is the reason that venison tallow produces a high quality soap. Nevertheless, you might want to make far more soap than a deer can produce (especially if the deer wasn't a fat one), and the way around this problem is to stretch your venison tallow supply with additions of other fats. Use the following listing to determine the proper mixing temperatures.

I have successfully made 100% venison soap with the tallow temperatures held at a low 120°F. but did note that an excessive formation of liquid glycerin also occurred. That was okay, except that it also meant that less actual soap was formed.

Virtually any animal fat or vegetable oil can be incorporated into soapmaking because these also will saponify to certain extents and to various degrees. Generally, fats with low melting points (such as

Soapmaking Temperatures for Various Fats

	Fat	*Lye Solution*
100% Venison Tallow	130–140°F.	100–105°F.
50% Tallow, 50% Beef Suet	125–135°F.	95–100°F.
100% Beef Suet	120–130°F.	90–95°F.
50% Beef Suet, 50% Pork Lard	100–110°F.	80–85°F.
100% Pork Lard	80–85°F.	70–75°F.

chicken fat) tend to detract from the quality of a soap and reduce the certainty of good results. Still, small amounts of coconut oil, palm oil, olive oil, and other similar ingredients have been used by modern soap manufacturers to improve the texture and character of some of their products and to make these soaps more appropriate for applications such as shampoos, laundry soaps, and dishwashing liquids.

Chapter 12

The Professional Trophy

Do You Really Want a Trophy Mount?

That's a fair question, but the answer might not always be immediately handy. Let's think about it for a minute. Is there something very special about the deer, or perhaps something unique about the actual hunting experience which led to its demise at your hand? A mounted deer head represents a frozen moment in time. The deer itself becomes literally immortalized, capable of provoking myriad visions of the autumn woodlands to all other hunters who behold the trophy. But when *you* are looking at the trophy, there will be only one vision there—the real one, the one that really happened. Perhaps the question regarding whether you really want a trophy mount should instead be this: will your life be enriched by reliving that moment in time several thousand times or more?

No trophy has ever been worn out by being looked at too many times. But there are many hunters whose appreciation for the magic of a particular moment has been worn thin by repeated exposure to the same old trophy head. Unless the antlers are of truly magnificent proportions, capable of demanding awe solely through their obvious superiority over most other deer, then it will have to be the hunting *experience* that justifies the mounting of a deer. In that case, if the experience was something less than a lifetime milestone, you should consider spending your money or time on something other than taxidermy. Sure, save the antlers and mount them on a plaque, or tan the hide and make something handsome and useful. But don't plan on enshrining a mounted deer head over the fireplace or on a living room wall unless the feat of your deer kill was a truly memorable event, one that filled you with exhilaration when it occurred. Otherwise, the trophy will be nothing other than a big hairy dust catcher (with antlers).

There is yet another popular justification for having a deer mounted into a trophy head, which is the old "conversation piece" argument. The reasoning is sometimes a little shaky, but the idea here is that a mounted trophy serves to give folks (particularly visitors) something to talk about, something by which they will be impressed. Aside from the fact that a pet tarantula or a shrunken head from the Amazon would serve this "conversation piece" purpose just as effectively, it should also be considered that the one person with whom you end up having the most conversation will probably be your spouse (or equivalent). Unless you possess a room or lair of your own where the mounted trophy can hang in unsullied splendor, then said spouse should have at least a two-thirds majority vote as to whether the deer will be mounted. If the living room decor is not compatible with shooting trophies, field trial ribbons, duck decoys, gun racks and bearskin rugs, neither will it be accommodating to a mounted deer head. No way, buddy. However, the wise and tactful hunter often can negotiate certain other favorable terms just by bringing up the subject of having a deer mounted. I know some fellows who reintroduce the subject every autumn; they lose out annually on the deer head proposal but win little concessions here and there which usually result in more hours of hunting unhindered by household chores. Life can be tough sometimes.

Under the right circumstances, a mounted trophy deer head is a truly handsome adornment, one which contributes to the overall appearance of a room. Modern professional taxidermy has attained such a high level of artistic proficiency that you half-expect to see a mounted deer flick an ear or blink an eye. Against a paneled wall, perhaps beside a gun cabinet or above a rustic fireplace, a mounted

deer head can be viewed both as a trophy and as a proper adornment to the room. If there will be no objections from other inhabi-
tants of that same room, and if either the hunting experience or the
size of the antler rack (or both) are deserving of being remembered,
then proceed with getting the deer mounted. After all, how often
do you drop a deer that truly qualifies for trophy status?

How to Get a Bigger Buck Next Year

Let's say that you only have room in the house for one deer mount.
Let's also say that your hunting budget is limited, and the cost of
having a deer mounted is an expense that you couldn't afford two
years in a row. Beginning to get the picture? The best way to insure
that you will get a bigger buck *next* year is to get *this* year's deer
mounted. It works like a charm, even better than wishing and hoping.

How to Postpone the Decision

There often are good reasons (other than simple indecision) for
postponing the final decision as to whether to get a certain deer
mounted. For one thing, that very special place on the wall where
a trophy could be appropriately hung might not even exist yet. The
den-of-your-own is perhaps still out there in the future, waiting for
the right combinations of time and money to occur. And speaking
of money, there just might not be enough of it right now to cover
the approximately one hundred dollars (plus or minus a couple of
tens) charged by most taxidermists. The list of possible postpone-
ments also includes the simple question whether the deer actually
qualifies as a trophy. Those of us who tend to be a trifle cynical even
during the moments of our own triumphs might prefer to let some
time pass in order to gain a more accurate perspective on the merits
of a so-called trophy.

For whichever reason that we might delay the decision whether
to have a deer mounted, the fact remains that delay can safely be
achieved with no adverse consequences. If certain measurements are
first taken and recorded, all we have to do is save the caped hide
and antlers in such a way that no spoilage or damage will occur to
them. Then, at a later date, we will still possess everything that is
required for a mount to be made. The skin and the antler cap—

that's all that the taxidermist uses from your deer when a mount is finally put together. If the deer skull has not been retained, then the original measurements will guide the taxidermist in the selection of a properly sized polystyrene mounting form.

The complete techniques for measuring and caping a deer for amateur taxidermy, which are the same techniques as for the proper field care of a trophy during extended away-from-home hunting trips, are described in chapter 13. For right now, however, we're looking at matters from the point of view that a professional taxidermist will eventually be doing the mounting. In fact, most taxidermists will perform any or all of the following steps listed below, steps which will permit you to delay the decision on whether to get the deer fully mounted. Just explain your situation, and I'm fairly certain that you will get all the needed cooperation for a very modest fee.

1. *A delay of a couple of months* can be achieved by merely placing the deer head (with shoulder hide attached) into a plastic bag, which is then put in the freezer. No salting is required. Some extra space can be saved by letting the antlers protrude from the plastic bag. However, the opening should be taped shut around the base of the antlers to avoid freezer burn on the hide.

2. *A delay of a year or so* also can be accomplished by freezing, but the extended storage time requires greater preparations. Completely cape the deer as described in chapter 13 (or pay a taxidermist to do it). This involves removing the hide from the skull. Remove cartilage from the ears by completely turning them inside out. Saw off the antler cap so that the antlers can be kept somewhere else besides in the freezer. Then wrap the hide and the skull separately and freeze. Again, no salting is required.

3. *A delay of several years,* or maybe even forever, is possible if the deerskin cape is first tanned and dried. The antlers are sawed from the skull and, if you wish, can be mounted on a plaque until the day arrives that you decide to have the cape and antlers put back together again as a full mount. You could store the skull in the freezer for several years, but if not, then take the appropriate measurements. The tanned hide will shrink, but it can later be soaked and then stretched back to the original size. Another option for a delay of several years is to save only the antlers; a cape from another deer (available through the taxidermist) can be substituted for the original at a later date.

A Visit to the Taxidermist

As deer season approaches, no hunter really knows for certain whether he or she will be successful in dropping a deer. That's why we call it hunting rather than slaughter; the evasive tactics used by the wily whitetail are, more often than not, able to foil our best strategies and plans. If we can't be the least bit certain that we will even see a deer within gun range, then our expectations for dropping a buck that qualifies for trophy status will be even less. (Or they should be, but hope always springs eternal.)

So, looking ahead to the oncoming season and perhaps getting somewhat excited as the autumn winds blow colder, yet not being assured of as much as a single forkful of venison, why should we consider visiting a taxidermist? Well, if we have in past years already dealt with a qualified taxidermist and have been pleased with the results, then we can forego this little expedition. This is a shopping trip of sorts that we're talking about. When that triumphant day finally arrives that a trophy buck is tagged with our name, a sudden and intense interest in taxidermy is sure to develop. It's best to enter into this rather exhilarating situation having already done a little groundwork. There are certain things that should be known about the quality of the work, the reliability, and the prices that can be expected. Another factor to consider is whether or not a certain taxidermist tends to be a specialist only in one field of taxidermy. He might have a grand reputation as a fish mounter, being gifted to perform all the careful artwork that is necessary to reproduce the natural colors of fish, and yet not have an artist's eye when it comes to the positioning and finishing work of deer mounting. A good reputation, passed along from one sportsperson to another, is the best form of advertising that a taxidermist can get. Query other hunters for their opinions on area taxidermists. Generally speaking, bad news carries faster and farther than good news, and you should be able to strike off certain names on your list of prospective taxidermists early in your investigations. But don't be too quick to react to an opinion that might easily be out-of-date and therefore obsolete. A bad experience (a poorly done mount) that happened five or ten years earlier might no longer be applicable. Skills increase with experience, and a taxidermist who earlier suffered under a poor reputation might be presently making up for it with super-quality work and very low prices.

Fig. 73. A taxidermist's workshop is a highly interesting place. Behind a huge pile of antlers, taxidermist Ted Wilson places a deer cape in a tanning barrel.

So, we are left with a trip to the taxidermist as still being the best way to evaluate the available services. And it's an enjoyable way to spend part of an afternoon because a taxidermy shop is one of the most interesting, if not downright fascinating, places on the face of the earth. Any excuse to visit such a place is a good one, so if you come prepared with intelligent questions about prices, options, specialities, and waiting times, your time will be particularly well spent. At any time of year, most taxidermists will have a variety of mounted fish and game on display. These generally are finished mounts that have not yet been claimed by their owners and, as such, represent a portion of the taxidermist's best efforts for the general public. Take a long gander at these. Do the deer mounts really look like normal deer? Seriously, the slightest offset in the positioning of a glass eye or the antlers can make a deer mount look awkward, if not grotesque. The position of the flared ears also can make or break the realistic appearance of a deer head. Such things are controlled by the taxidermist in the final finishing stages of mounting, and if he or she lacks a naturalist's eye and an artist's skills, the mounts will betray that lack. Inspect the mounts for less obvious flaws, such as gaps where the hide butts up against the base of the antlers, and visible stitches where the mouth has been sewn. A deer's nose and the membranes around the eyes should have a moist appearance due to the artful application of oil paints to achieve this effect. All in all, a deer mount should appear alert, yet not give the impression of being wide-eyed and fearful. On the opposite hand, some poorly done mounts appear so complacent and sleepy-eyed that you are reminded of domestic animals lazily chewing their cuds.

Don't be shy about asking questions, even to the point of asking for a guided tour of the facilities. As I indicated earlier, a taxidermy workshop is a highly interesting place, virtually a treasure house of gamebird, mammal, and fish mounts in various stages of completion, piles of antlers, also snakeskins, miscellaneous furs and tanned hides, grizzly skulls, and many other kinds of similarly neat stuff that appeals to the curious hunter and natural history buff. There often is a cracker-barrel atmosphere that prevails at a taxidermist's workshop, one which attracts the "good old boys" who are never short of at least one more deer story to tell. Under circumstances like this, it can be difficult for a taxidermist to perform an honest day's work. Remember this so that you can depart before the welcome has worn thin. Intelligent and well-directed questions will always be answered, but don't regale the taxidermist with endless tales of your hunting exploits. The taxidermist usually hears more deer stories in a single year than you will in an entire lifetime. Show mercy; limit yourself to only one whitetail adventure (preferably a true one). Then skedaddle.

What the Taxidermist Can Do for You

The services offered by most qualified taxidermists are much wider in scope than hunters probably realize. Sure, pure-and-simple mounting is the chief business in which these professionals are engaged, but nevertheless there are many other services also available to meet customers' varied needs. Knowing that such services exist can help you to make wiser decisions regarding the preservation and full utilization of your hunting trophies.

— *Antler repair* can be performed by most taxidermists so that an otherwise ruined trophy can be mounted in unspoiled splendor. Missing tines can be replaced so effectively that you would be hard pressed to tell which of them was "fake." As with silk purses and sow's ears, a trophy rack cannot be manufactured from a mediocre rack, but short of that miracle, damaged antlers can usually be returned to their original glory.

— *Rough caping* of the original deer carcass is a chore that many hunters would just as soon pass along to a professional. Although the skinning and rough caping of a deer is no more difficult than changing a flat tire, you don't need to feel guilty about having this chore done by the taxidermist who will do the mounting. It's part of his job, and he certainly can do it faster and better than you could. First make arrangements by telephone and then simply transport the whole deer to the workshop.

— *Reconditioning* can often revive the original splendor of an otherwise moth-eaten and decrepit whitetail trophy mount. Poorly done mounts, and those which were assembled decades ago without the benefits of modern taxidermy methods, often

Fig. 74. A wide variety of positions and mounting styles are available, including head mounts, neck mounts, and full shoulder-length mounts.

will show a general deterioration. For example, a hide that had been excessively stretched to cover too big a mounting form may show signs of shrinking and cracking. Oftentimes, the original hide can be removed for repairs and even additional tanning. However, hair shedding cannot be stopped, and if that is the case, a brand new cape must be substituted. Taxidermists can obtain capes through various supply houses, but you might want to provide your own, using the head and neck skin from a large doe or from a buck with less than trophy-size antlers.

—*Hide tanning* services can be obtained through most taxidermists, and some actually do the work themselves rather than send hides elsewhere to be tanned. Hides can be tanned with the hair left on or removed, depending upon whether you want to use them as "trophy" blankets or for cutting into leathercraft items. Many taxidermists also buy green hides from hunters, which they then sell in large lots to leather producers.

—*Leathercraft* is often practiced as a sideline by many taxidermists, and a variety of leather working tools, handicraft items, and the leather itself can be purchased from them. Even if a particular taxidermist is not directly involved with leathercraft, he usually can tell you where to go for whatever you need. Generally, any taxidermist in deer country can arrange to provide you with tanned leather if you make your needs known in advance. Also, if you want to have deerhides fabricated into vests, jackets or other items, a taxidermist can usually arrange to provide this service, either directly or indirectly.

—*Specialty items* such as deer-leg gun racks, lamp mounts, antler mounts, and almost any other variation or novelty version of taxidermy can be created by a taxidermist. Many specialty items such as antler mounts are standard to the industry and therefore are relatively inexpensive. Custom jobs that require extra time and care will cost extra. To find out which is which, you'll have to ask the taxidermist, because each has his own specialties.

—*Advice* is something you only want to receive from experts, and a taxidermist is obviously qualified to advise you on the selec-

Fig. 75. A deer foot lamp mount is one of the specialty items done by most taxidermists.

tion of mounting styles and positions. I have found that taxidermists are often reluctant to provide unsolicited advice, apparently desiring to avoid talking a customer into something that he or she might not really like. However, sincere requests for recommendations will usually be rewarded with answers. A taxidermist can take one quick glance at a trophy deer head and know immediately whether an upright or head-extended position would best compliment the antlers. The location where the finished trophy will be hung has considerable bearing on whether the mount should face left, right, or straight ahead, and a taxidermist can key you in on some of these factors. Some styles of deer mounts look better on a wood plaque, while others are best left unadorned. Any experienced taxidermist has seen many deer mounts come and go, so he consequently knows what looks good and what doesn't.

— *Super-quality mounting* for an extra fee is sometimes offered by expert taxidermists. This fact deserves an explanation because most of us tend to think that the very best is what we automatically get. T'aint so; what we get when we pay regular prices is regular quality. The vast majority of professionally done deer mounts are performed using standard polyethylene head forms, medium grade glass eyes, and a minimum of time and effort. Like most of us, a taxidermist has to cut his or her own expenses and also cannot afford to dally over finishing touches that would go largely unrecognized and unappreciated by the general public. However, the discerning whitetail trophy hunter willing to pay a higher fee can usually obtain custom mounting of competition-grade quality. For example, glass eyes that have veined irises and a more natural looking bluish glint in the pupils are more expensive, but they provide a deer mount with a startling vitality. Custom-made head and shoulder forms are more apt to exactly match the true size of the original deer and also can strike postures far different from the standard factory models. The extra work involved with building up certain underlying areas of the form to achieve a more lifelike expression and overall appearance requires a lot of time and refitting. You can expect to pay at least twice the usual fee for full competition-grade deer mounting. But the chief obstacle is in finding a taxidermist who will agree to do all this extra work for such small payment!

Care and Cleaning of Whitetail Trophy Mounts

We tend to think of a deer mount as something that escapes the ravages of time, something which has been endowed by the taxidermist's alchemy with a piece of eternity. That concept does, in fact, contain a certain validity in that a properly preserved whitetail mount will last for a very, very long time. How long? Well, long enough that we don't really need to know the answer to that question. (Never will, either.) Still, let's not get the idea that a deer mount has the ageless durability of a statue struck in bronze or chiseled from granite. Even a deer's antlers are subject to change; they shrink 5-8 percent in the first year before all the contained moistures are finally gone. (This means that a regal twenty-inch spread can be reduced by at least an inch. Ouch!) The hide of a mount is resistant to bacterial growth, but it is not preserved against the elements of heat and humidity. The natural color of the hair will fade in direct sunlight and can be discolored by woodsmoke and tobacco fumes. And, as a dust catcher, a deer mount could win prizes. A dirty, dusty, discolored, cracked, and faded trophy is not what we had in mind, however, when we took that original ride to the taxidermist's shop. With just a minimum of care and periodic cleaning, a whitetail trophy will continue to have that same sparkling vitality.

Ordinary dusting can do much to maintain a general good appearance. A friend of mine, while visiting elsewhere, spotted a deer mount that apparently was a buck still in velvet; that is, the antlers had the soft, thickened appearance typical of those seen on late summer bucks. My friend moved closer to inspect this unusual trophy and was forming the words to question his host about the "velvet" when he realized that it was just a collection of dust. Although you and I (of course!) would never let a trophy deteriorate to this extreme, the cold fact remains that a subtle change in a trophy is difficult to detect. We glance at it at least a dozen times a day and see no more dust or grime in the evening than was there in the morning — or so we think.

If the trophy is to be taken down off its wall moorings for a more thorough cleaning, carry it only by grasping the throat and the base of the mount. Don't lug it by the antlers because these are not always as securely fastened as you might think. Forget those memories of dragging the deer from the woods by the antlers, at least temporarily.

How to Clean a Trophy

Gentle vacuuming will suck out deeply embedded dust particles that ordinary dusting can't reach. However, go easy with vacuuming; deer hair is brittle, and it can break off if the nozzle is stroked too briskly across the trophy.

A buildup of grease and grime can be removed by washing the trophy with just about any of the cold-water soaps and cleaning agents that are specified for fine fabrics. Once again the word "gentle" is needed. A properly tanned trophy hide can withstand a fair amount of rigorous washing, but nevertheless there is a limit to the abuse which a trophy can take. Ideally, the liquid washing solution should be applied with a spray bottle so that excessive amounts of water do not soak through to the hide. Comb the wetted hairs to slick the grime off, stroking with the grain, not against it. Rinsing is also needed to remove both the soap and the dirt that it now carries. Before the trophy is allowed to dry, comb the hairs back into the proper and natural alignment. No styling, please. Let the trophy dry slowly in an area where air can circulate. Don't use a hair dryer or any other heat source. Finally, a quick once-over with the vacuum cleaner will fluff up the hairs and separate those which might have stuck together.

Extra Touch-Ups for Trophies

A mounted whitetail trophy will usually have had a black oil paint or other coating applied to the nose and the tear ducts of the eyes to simulate a naturally moist appearance. As the years pass, the coating sometimes weathers and deteriorates so that a dull, dry look takes over. Antlers also lose some of the natural polish that was originally put there by the buck itself in battles with bushes while removing the velvet of summer. The antlers gradually oxidize on the surface so that a chalky dullness eventually replaces the natural glint.

The nose, tear ducts, and antlers can all be restored with an application of clear varnish. A fine-tipped artist's brush works best for the more detailed painting of the nose and eyes, but a small rag will work nicely for applying varnish to the antlers. In place of varnish, a mixture of one part linseed oil and three parts turpentine can be substituted to achieve a more subdued natural luster. Older, more oxidized antlers may require a second application. Small cracks in the nose and around the eyelids can be filled with shoe polish wax. Apply a drop or two of ammonia window-cleaning solution to each glass eye and gently wipe clean. Oftentimes, a film of tobacco or woodsmoke will have obscured the original gleam.

Before the trophy is hung back on the wall, check both the base hanger and the wall anchor to insure that a sturdy connection still exists.

Chapter 13

"Do-It-Yourself" Taxidermy

Amateur Means "Lover"

Amateur taxidermy can range from the very simple task of attaching antlers to a plaque on through to the full scale preparation and mounting of a deer head. For the do-it-yourselfer who has somewhat of an artistic bent and a pair of skilled hands, amateur taxidermy can produce satisfactory results on the very first attempt. Oftentimes, the only real difference between the work done by a well-informed amateur and the same job done by an experienced professional is that the amateur usually takes longer to do it right. (A *lot* longer!) But that's all right: amateur taxidermy can be a very enjoyable hobby. In fact, the word "amateur" springs from a more ancient one that meant "lover." If you don't truly love messing around with animal skins and bones and other interesting stuff like that in order to create an end product having a natural beauty of its own, then forget amateur taxidermy. Leave it in the hands of the professionals. But remember, the work that goes into creating a trophy becomes an intrinsic part of what that trophy will mean to its owner as the years pass. If the thought of doing your own taxidermy is appealing, the following pages describe how to prepare some of the standard types of whitetail trophies.

Antler Mounts

By far the most common trophy of the whitetail deer is a set of antlers. Too often, these handsome ornaments are merely rough-sawed from the head and then are nailed to a garage wall or above a barn door, or are tossed up on a shelf and soon forgotten. With just a little extra effort, antlers can be mounted onto an attractive varnished wood plaque so that they can more properly be displayed on a den wall or above a fireplace. With a leather or copper sheeting cover over the attached skull plate, mounted antlers become trophies. If lacking this good and respectful treatment, antlers are no more than tacky souveniers.

Removing Antlers from Deer

A set of antlers can be removed from a deer as one intact unit held together by a portion of the top of the skull. An ordinary hacksaw or carpenter's crosscut saw are adequate for this job, which takes less than a few minutes to complete. Sawing will be easier if you first cut the hide with a knife along the path you intend the saw to follow. Begin at a point about two inches to the rear of the antlers and aim for a point an inch or so in front of them, which is usually just above the eyes of the average sized buck. Try to complete this job in one straight cut; some folks make a second cut down through the deer's forehead, but this later makes the antler mounting into a more difficult task.

When the antlers are freed from the deer, remove the hide with a pair of pliers and trim away any bits of flesh that might still be adhered. No chemical preservatives are required. You might find that fragments of tree bark and gummy resins are embedded in the knurled base of each antler, and these can be removed with gasoline and a wire brush. If excessive cleaning turns the antlers too white, the natural color can be restored with thinned woodstain.

Attaching Antlers to a Plaque

Unfinished wood plaques can be purchased at hobby and craft stores. Antlers usually have a better appearance if mounted on small plaques less than eight inches wide; our imaginative eye is forever trying to create the image of the deer's head behind a set of antlers, and the outline of the plaque helps satisfy that striving. If an oval plaque is used, arrange it for hanging vertically and plan to attach the antlers slightly above the halfway point. The traditional outline of a shield (as in a coat of arms) is particularly suitable for antler mounting.

Now cut a more or less circular piece of three-quarter-inch wood that is slightly larger than the skull plate. This will fit between the skull plate and the plaque and will provide a raised edge for the fastening of the leather, velvet, copper sheeting, or whatever will be later used to cover the skull plate.

Before doing any permanent fastening, check the angle that the antlers will display by holding everything together against a wall. As a rule of thumb, the outer tips of the main beams should not hang lower than where the antlers attach to the skull plate. Otherwise, they will appear to droop. On the other hand, if the tines are positioned too far upright, the mounted set will forever beg the observer's eye to create a conspiciously absent deer's head. If any shimming needs to be done, this is the time to do it. Finally, assemble the antlers, wood inset, and plaque with screws. Cut the leather or other covering to size and check for fit. You might elect to build up the skull plate with papier-maché or modeling clay to achieve a more natural contour. Then tack the covering into place with brass tacks. Another equally effective means of covering the antler base can be accomplished solely with papier-maché if it is later painted to a suitable dark flat brown color.

Antler and Deer Leg Gun Rack Mounts

The lower legs and hooves of a deer are relatively resistant to spoilage and can be made into gun rack supports, lamp shades, hassock legs, and other novelty items with a minimum of preparation. These parts of a deer, which are routinely removed in the first steps of skinning, contain so little flesh that a deer is literally immune

Fig. 76. Next to a full head mount, an antler mount is the most common way the successful hunter displays his trophy.

to rattlesnake bite near ground level. Some taxidermists use virtually no chemical preservatives at all for the mounting of deer legs. Others, like Ted Wilson – who was my mentor for these last two chapters – claim that nothing short of full tanning will preserve deer legs for protection over the long haul against bugs and hair fallout. After getting so much other good advice from Ted, it would be foolish of me to in turn recommend anything less than complete tanning. Certainly, if you are planning to tan the entire deer hide, it's no extra effort to toss the legs in with it. I will tell you, though, about a certain deer leg that I've been trying to get rid of for the last three years. I've given it the heave-ho many times out behind the barn, but inevitably one of the local cats brings it back inside. Let me tell you, that boomerang leg is still in good shape, smells all right, and still has all its hair. (Don't ask me why the cats do that; so far they've done nothing but retrieve it.) Of course, you want a gun rack or other

Fig. 77. For a truly professional deer leg rack mount, skin the leg to the hoof, sever the lowest joint at the hoof, and remove and discard the bones. Later, replace them with a mounting form.

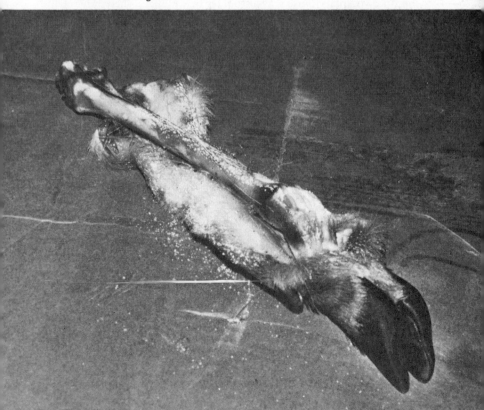

deer leg construction to last far longer than three years or so. Let's do the job right and not compromise.

A truly professional deer leg mount is done by skinning the leg all the way down to the hoof, at which point the lowest joint is severed (right at the hoof) and the bones are removed and discarded. A precast form is then substituted for the leg bones after the hide, with hoof attached, has been tanned. These forms are "L" shaped for holding guns and have a threaded rod inserted into one end for attachment to the wall plaque. The hide is then sewn into place around the form and the deer leg mount is finished.

The amateur taxidermist, lacking easy access to forms, can accomplish the same objective by leaving the original leg bone intact and still attached to the hoof. The skinning should still be done so that any flesh can be removed and so the hide will be better exposed for tanning (see chapter 10 for home-tanning procedures). If the leg is to be used as part of a gun rack, it should be bent at the joint into the "L" position after tanning and kept that way until the sinews dry and take a firm set. Obviously, if you don't want the leg bent because you plan to use it as a stool leg or whatever, then don't bend it. Finally, fill in around the bone with modeling clay to replace any discarded flesh so that the hide can be neatly fitted and sewn back into place around the leg bones. Now drill a hole into the marrow of the exposed end of the leg bone for inserting a threaded bolt. Counter bore the backside of the wall plaque to accommodate the head of the bolt if you're planning to assemble an authentic whitetail country gun rack, or fasten in other ways according to the type of object you are creating. A squirt of epoxy glue in the hole of the bone will help hold the bolt in place. Hooves can be made bright and shiny with a drop or two of linseed oil.

European-Style Head Mounting

Here's a unique and yet simple method for mounting a trophy deer head. The European-style mount consists of no more than the deer's skull, minus the jawbone and modified so that it will hang flush against a wall or wood plaque. The antlers are left attached to the skull and are sometimes polished or rubbed with linseed oil so that a rich luster is provided for contrast with the bleached snowy

Fig. 78. The finished mount. One like this can easily be made by an amateur
taxidermist.

white of the skull. A whitetail trophy displayed in this manner has a very striking appearance and admittedly not one that has an appeal to all viewers. The European mount is an artifact rather than art and more beast than beauty. It looks better in a rustic setting, such as in a den or a hunting camp, than it does hung over the television set in the living room. The ideal setting for a European-style mount is in the great hall of a baronial estate, where the flickering glow of a fireplace illuminates walls festooned with broadswords, shields, and the antlers of mighty stags that cast dancing shadows on the beams overhead. If we must temporarily settle for a somewhat less grand arrangement than a baronial hall, we at least can appreciate the origins of this type of trophy mount.

By one way of thinking, the European skull mount is a more interesting and authentic relic of the whitetail hunt than is a "living" full shoulder mount constructed with a polystyrene form, a tanned hide, oil paint makeup, and a couple of glass eyeballs. The bare skull has a realism that can't be ignored. A European mount also has the advantage of making the antlers appear larger and thus more impressive because the thick hair and wide flared ears are not present to diminish the sweep of the antlers. One optional modification of the European mount involves covering the skull with the original skin, which is tanned with the hair still attached. Traditionally, the eyes are sewn shut and the ears are omitted.

Step 1—Removing the Skull

The portion of the skull that will be mounted is best removed with a crosscut saw or hacksaw. Deerhide is remarkably resistant to sawing, so either first skin the head completely or else cut through the hide along the path that the saw will be following. Start at a point a little over two inches behind the antler base and aim for the corners of the mouth. This defines a path that will take your saw just below the eye sockets. It's better to saw off a slightly larger skull section than what will be mounted because the excess bone can later be trimmed more accurately to achieve a flat base. Finally, when the sawing is finished, pull off the skin and remove the brain in preparation for the next step.

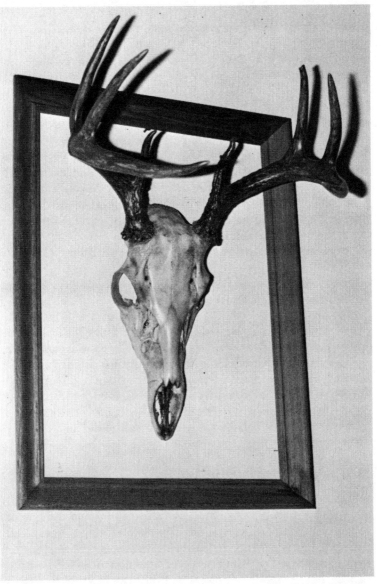

Fig. 79. The European-style head mount is an interesting alternative to full mount-ing, more bestial than beautiful. The author plans to eventually fasten this skull to a polished wood plaque or a black velvet background.

Step 2—Cleaning the Skull

Most of the raw flesh and tissue should be left on the skull until soaking or boiling renders it to a more tender consistency. The reasoning here is that the bone structure of the exposed sinus and nasal passages is very fragile and can be easily chipped and otherwise damaged during the removal of adhered flesh. Boiling is probably the cleanest and least messy way to soften the flesh, but finding a container that is just the right size can be a problem. The skull needs to be submerged up to the base of the antlers, but most pots and pans are too small for this because the antlers will span the sides and prevent a full submersion. A turkey roasting pan, even one of the disposable aluminum varieties, can usually be commandeered into service to get this job done. Boil for several hours and then remove, cool, and clean the skull. A second boiling will usually free whatever tissue might remain.

Soaking in cold water can also produce a remarkably clean skull, but several weeks of soaking are required for effective results. Consequently, the last stages of cleaning by hand will be somewhat odoriferous—that is, downright "smelly".

Some hunters figure that they can get a clean deer skull just by placing it on an anthill or by tacking it up on a barn wall where the yellow jackets can do their thing. These might seem like good ideas, but they never really work, at least not for the first two or three years of exposure. Two of the drawbacks to these let-nature-do-it methods are that (1) once the flesh dries and hardens, even the insects can't pull it free, and (2) while the skull is weathering, so are the antlers, which can soon be damaged beyond an acceptable limit.

Step 3—Bleaching

Ordinary liquid laundry bleach can be used to whiten the skull, although hydrogen peroxide can be substituted for somewhat quicker results and a milder chemical odor. When bleaching the deer skull that hangs in my den (nope, no baronial estate here either), I merely applied bleach with a paint brush every half hour or so for the better part of an afternoon and then rinsed the skull in water to remove the crystalline powder that had formed on it during evaporation of the bleach liquid. The effect was striking; the bone had become a snowy white. I had also bleached the antlers, which also were pure white, but I later applied wood stain and varnish to return them to a more natural appearance.

Step 4—Fitting and Hanging

The bottom side of the skull, where the original sawcut was made, should be perfectly flat so that it will fit flush against the wall or on a wood plaque. Usually a certain amount of sanding is required, and a belt sander will give the best results. Be careful that you don't snap the more fragile bones when pressure is applied for sanding.

When flatness is finally achieved, your European-style head mount can be hung on a bare wall simply by propping the rear edge of the skull over a hanger. Sometimes it is necessary to first carve a little notch on the inside of the skull to get a more secure connection with the hanger. If a picture frame is similarly hung around the skull mount, it will help highlight the trophy.

A more permanent means of displaying the trophy, one which also provides a handsome and more secure means of hanging, involves attaching the skull to a stained and varnished wood plaque. This can be done by means of a single bolt. There is a shelf of bone that extends partway across the brain cavity on the underside of the skull, and this can be drilled with a single hole to accommodate the bolt. To determine the location of the corresponding hole on the plaque, first trace the outline of the skull on a piece of paper. Cut this template out and punch a hole in the paper where the drilled hole is. Position the template over the plaque where it looks the best and make a mark where the hole in the plaque should be. Drill this hole and counterbore the backside of the plaque to accommodate the nut. Insert the bolt from inside the brain cavity on through the plaque and twist on the nut until finger-tight.

The outline of the plaque can do much to enhance the appearance of the European-style trophy. However, a plaque that is too large will detract from it. Select, or make, one which extends not much more than an inch from underneath all sides of the skull. As with bare antler mounts, the viewer's eye needs to see something which suggests the outline of a deer's head. The skull does part of this, but a poorly chosen plaque can offset even that advantage. If in

doubt, settle for an oval-shaped plaque that is about six inches wide
and twelve inches high.

How to Do a Full Mount

The traditional full mounting of a deer's head, neck, and shoulders is usually left to the hands of the professional taxidermists, but
this doesn't mean that *you* can't do it too! While it is usually true
that the professional is better equipped to perform such a task, the
fact remains that an amateur can gather together enough of the right
tools, equipment, and enthusiasm to tackle full mounting and get
results that are just as good. If nothing else, the amateur has the
element of spare time on his or her side, and there's nothing else
that's more important when you're striving for perfection.

The following pages will tell you all you need to know about performing a full whitetail head mount. There is not a single step in
the mounting process that is any more difficult than, say, cleaning
a rifle or skinning a deer. Like so many other seemingly complex
jobs, deer mounting can be broken down into easily understood and
easily done steps.

Tools and Equipment

Only the original hide, the antlers, and a piece of skull bone attached to the antlers are removed from the deer for mounting. The
beauty of modern taxidermy is only skin-deep; all the other materials
used in a deer mount are synthetic.

Fully half the work of mounting a deer goes into tanning the
portion of the hide that will cover the head and neck. Even most
professional taxidermists farm this task out to the leather tanning
industries. So, unless you are already planning to tan the rest of the
deerhide anyway, consider having the cape tanned by others. Even
with the cost of this added to what you will need to pay for taxidermy supplies, a do-it-yourself mounting will usually cost less than
half what a professional would charge. (That's because your time
is free, but a taxidermist's isn't.) The following list shows all the
materials that you will need for doing a full mount:

- Tanning chemicals (optional)
- Wood plaque (optional)
- Polystyrene mounting form
- Ear liners
- Glass eyes
- Modeling clay
- Curved surgical needle
- Waxed nylon thread
- Black wax shoe polish
- Black oil paint and artist's brush
- Assorted tacks and pins
- Spring-loaded clothes pins

All of the necessary materials can be obtained through one or more of the various taxidermy mail-order houses that service amateurs as well as professionals. Most of these outfits advertise in the back pages of the outdoor magazines. You might even be able to talk a professional taxidermist into supplying what you need—for a fee, of course.

The mounting form is the virtual foundation on which the success of your mounting endeavors will ride. Usually made from polystyrene foam (and sometimes from compressed paper), the mounting form resembles the skinned head and neck of a deer, with the top of the head cut away to accommodate the skull cap and antlers. The form also contains a wood base in the head and on the surface that contacts the wall. According to Ted Wilson—who unlocked many of the mysteries of taxidermy for me—mounting forms come in two sizes: too small and too big. To achieve a good fit with the hide, considerable sanding and/or building up is often required.

You can, of course, make your own mounting form from papier-maché by using the original skull, boiled clean, and with the jawbone wired into position. In this situation, the antlers can be left attached to the skull, and there obviously will be no question regarding their proper position. However, take very good measurements of the deer's neck and shoulders for later reconstruction. By making your own form, virtually any position of the deer's head can be obtained. Commercially, the only options generally are to have the deer turned left, turned right, facing straight ahead, or lowered into the "sneak" position, where the left or right positions are sometimes not available.

In all of these categories, you often can select either the shorter neck length or the full-size neck and shoulder-length form.

There are no substitutes for glass eyes. Pay a couple of dollars extra and get the best quality eyes that you can find. (As amateurs, we need all the help we can get.)

Ear liners are flexible plastic inserts that help hold the ears in proper position. These can be made from sheet metal using the original ear cartilage as a template, but the price for commercial liners is so low that purchasing them is probably the best thing to do.

Ordinary modeling clay—such as is supplied to children to keep them out of your hair—and black wax shoe polish are used to fill in around and under the ears, eyes, and nose. Black oil paint serves to color the nose and tear ducts.

Measurements

Before the deer is skinned and caped, certain measurements should be taken to aid in selecting the right size mounting form and in the accurate reconstruction of the deer's profile. The importance of these measurements tends to be overrated (many professionals don't even bother with them), but there is no denying the usefulness of good measurements as an aid to inexperienced amateurs.

The three measurements that are most often used for classifying deer mounting forms by size are shown below. The "A" and "B" measurements are taken before the deer is skinned, and "C" is taken after skinning.

"A"—Tip of nose to back center of skull.
"B"—Tip of nose to forward corner of eye.
"C"—Circumference of neck, just below head.

Two other dimensions that will greatly aid in the accurate positioning of the antlers on the mounting form are (1) the distance between the tip of each antler and the nose, and (2) the distance of each antler base from the nose.

Caping the Deer

There is a standard procedure for removing the hide and antlers from a whitetail deer that is used almost universally by guides, outfitters, trophy hunters, and taxidermists. This method, called "caping," consists of skinning the deer from the shoulders to the tip of the nose using only two major cuts with the skinning knife. The antlers are then removed by sawing off the top of the skull.

Most hunters never have to perform a full caping in order to have a deer mounted because this is done as a service by the taxidermist. If you can transport just the unskinned head (with shoulder and neck hide still attached) to a taxidermist within a couple days of the kill, there is no need to know how to fully cape a deer. But if you are hunting in a remote area and have cause for concern that the trophy might begin to deteriorate before it arrived at a taxidermist's shop, then the deer should be caped so that salting can be done. The same caping technique is used for both amateur and professional taxidermy, so if you're planning to mount a deer, you'll have to do the caping.

A deer can be caped either on the ground, or hung head-down from a hoist. Most writers on this subject suggest that the first cut be made around the shoulders and chest so that the cape can then be peeled down and over the head. However, you have to eventually skin the whole deer anyway, so why not make caping the *last* part of the skinning chore? Begin skinning at the rear legs in the head-down position and peel the skin as far down as the deer's shoulders. The fold of the hide where it encircles the shoulders and chest will present you with an opportunity to make the first caping cut from the *flesh* side of the hide. This way, you avoid having to cut through hair to get to the hide. The fold of the inside out hide will also give your knife a true, circular path to follow around the deer's chest and shoulders. You want to leave plenty of hide with the cape. Any surplus can always be trimmed later when the mount is fitted to the mounting form.

Once this cut has been made, the hide from the back and rear quarters will fall free from the carcass. All the hide that now remains attached to the deer is the cape. Before removing the cape, first make a cut in the hide from the middle of the shoulders to the back of the antlers. This cut should be reasonably straight and true over the full length of the back of the neck. At the bottom end of the cut, it should fork into a "Y," the points of which end at the bases of the two antlers.

Now the cape can be peeled down over the neck until the base

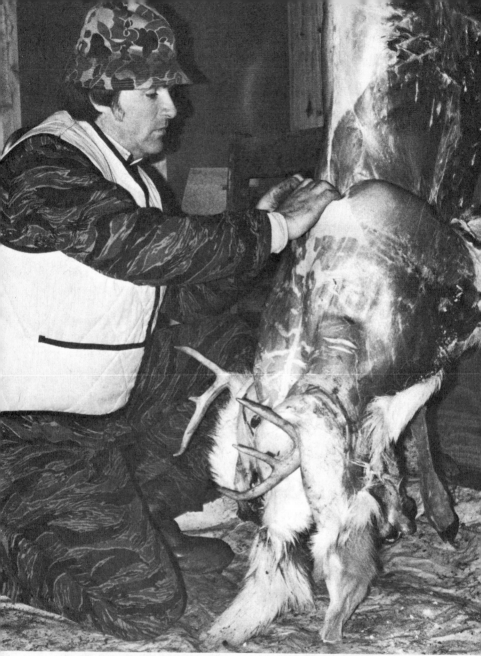

Fig. 80. Caping can be done more easily if the hide is first peeled down from the hindquarters. At the location shown in the photo, the first caping cut can be made from the flesh side of the hide. (Congratulations Bill Sheesley; that buck has a nice rack.)

of the head is reached. The neck can now be severed so that the skinning of the head can be done elsewhere. If you do that, the deer has been "rough-caped," which is the condition that most trophies are in when transported to a professional taxidermist. But, in this chapter, *you* are the taxidermist, so let's keep working.

So, you can either finish caping the head while it's still attached to the carcass or removed for easier access. Makes no difference; either way has its merits. Peel the hide from around the base of each antler. This can be difficult because the hide is firmly attached here. Don't use the knife. Ironically, a blunt screwdriver seems to work better than anything for prying the hide loose.

The cartilage at the base of each ear is deeply embedded in a recess, and you should remove it intact so as to avoid cutting through to the visible interior of the ear. The cartilage can be left attached to the hide, at least for now.

Skinning around the eyes requires great care but not great skill. Just be sure that you don't accidentally slice through the eyelids or tear ducts because these are needed for a realistic mount. With one hand, grasp an eyelid between two fingers so that you can pull it gently away from the carcass while the other hand makes the necessary cuts from the flesh side of the hide.

Finally, we arrive at the nose and lips. You have to be twice as careful here because the inside out appearance of the deer is deceptive. For example, the hide on the lips actually extends partway into the mouth, and you'll need to leave this attached to the cape for later sewing the mouth shut. Similarly, the considerable bulk of cartilage underlying the nose is also part of the internal structure of the nostrils and cannot all be removed without disfiguring the cape. This is no time to pick up speed.

At last the cape will be separated from the carcass. Now the ears have to be turned inside out so that they will be more effectively exposed for salting and tanning. This maneuver is a trifle troublesome because each ear contains a rigid flap of cartilage that should only partially be removed. The cartilage helps protect the velvety inner lining of the ear during tanning, so it only needs to be parted from the hide of the back of the ear. To do this, gently slip a blunt instrument such as a butter knife up behind the cartilage until enough separation has occurred that the ear can be turned inside out like a sock.

Fig. 81. Here's the completely inverted cape, sans skull and ready for tanning.

The entire cape should be thoroughly salted and rolled into a bundle for temporary storage. If there will be a delay before tanning, salt again a day later after shaking the original salt loose. Salt draws moisture from the hide and needs to be replaced if it gets soggy. (See chapter 10 for instructions for tanning.)

Remove the antlers from the skull by sawing off the one bone cap to which they are both attached. The type of saw cut that you make will depend on the design of the mounting form that you will be using. If the entire top of the head of the mounting form is flat, then saw from the rear point of the skull straight through the middle of the eyeballs. (Taxidermy has no room for squeamish folks.) If the form is notched on top, then start the saw cut in the same direction as was just described but stop short of the eyes. Then make a second cut through the forehead down to the first cut and the antlers can be lifted from the deer.

Assembling the Mount

This is the part where it all comes together. Assembling the tanned cape, antlers, and eyes is really no more difficult than was the original caping job; that is, the assembling will proceed smoothly if the fit is good so you don't have to spend a lot of time shimming and shaving. In either case, a little patience will carry you a long way towards the successful completion of a handsome trophy mount.

Step 1—Prop the antlers on the mounting form and check for fit. You might have to trim off some of the skull cap, or possibly insert a wood wedge or two, before the positioned antlers satisfy the measurements (to the tip of the nose) that were taken before caping. There is a wiggly seam in the center of the skull cap; make sure that it is centered with the cast seam of the mounting form. Finally, attach firmly by putting two or three wood screws through the skull cap into the wood block that is embedded in the form. Fill in any gaps that exist with modeling clay until the head has an appropriate deer-like profile.

Depending on the type of mounting form that you have, it might be necessary to cut a slot in the form where the mouth would normally open. This slot will later be used to grip the inner edges of the lips and mouth area.

Step 2—If the tanned cape is stiff and dry, soak in water until

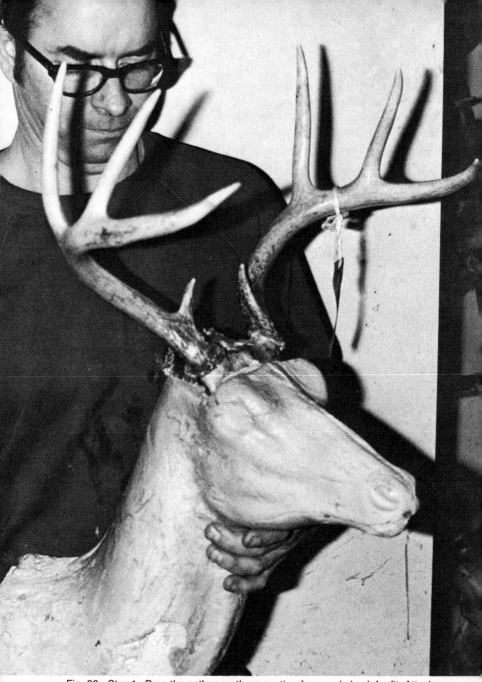

Fig. 82. *Step 1*—Prop the antlers on the mounting form and check for fit. Attach with screws to the wood base of the "head."

it is pliable and relaxed. The cape will have shrunk somewhat during tanning, but it can be stretched back to normal size to fit the form. Actually, it can be stretched to temporarily fit a too-large form, but don't do that, because the skin would otherwise crack at a later date. When the ear cartilages are pliable (they might require a little extra soaking), peel them off. However, don't remove the bulky base of the ear. Insert the plastic ear liners in place of the cartilage and check for fit. The skin within the cup of each ear should be able to easily fit against the liner. If it doesn't, trim off the edges of the liner until it does. Application of a water-base glue (such as dextrin) to the ear liners and the mounting form will help hold the hide in position on the finished mount.

Place the cape on the mounting form and locate it relative to the eye depressions and the antler beams. Drive a few small nails here and there to temporarily hold the cape in place, but only put them partway in so they can later be removed. Check to make certain that the neck hide is not twisted or off center. Pull and tug here and there,

Fig. 83. *Step 2*—A deer's ear turned inside out and the plastic ear liner that will replace the original cartilage.

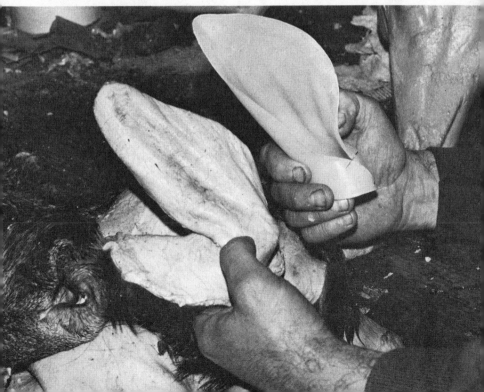

drive a few more nails, and look for realism more than anything else in your assessment of whether the hide fits the mold. If you're not satisfied, do it over again. A poor fit means a poor mount.

Step 3—Get out the needle and thread, preferably a curved surgical needle and strong nylon thread. All stitches that you make should be from under the skin towards the outside surface so that hair doesn't get pulled down into the loops of the thread. Start sewing near the base of one antler and sew to the junction of the "Y" incision. Then do the other side. Tie securely and then proceed on down the back of the neck. Considerable force is sometimes necessary to get the two sides of the cape to join in a single seam. An extra pair of hands here will be appreciated. You might have to slip the hide just a bit towards the head to get a tight seam. Continue on about an inch past the form. Any excess hide should be trimmed off about

Fig. 84. *Step 3*—Place the tanned cape on the mounting form and check for fit. Begin sewing at base of antlers. Use nails to hold cape in place until sewing is finished.

Fig. 85. The mount has been pinned and clipped into position for drying. Paint and wax have not yet been applied to the eyes and nose.

a couple of inches past the butt end of the form. Fold it over and staple into place especially if glue was applied earlier.

Step 4—Attach a hanger to the backplate of the mounting form so that you can hang the trophy for easier access to the facial area. Force the lip linings into the mouth slot with a screwdriver and pin the mouth into place. Use a lot of pins to resist shrinkage during drying. Place a wad of paper in each nostril to prevent them from distorting during drying. Place some modeling clay in the eye sockets and then insert the glass eyes. Remember, a deer has elliptical pupils which are aligned horizontally. Arrange the eyelids into a realistic expression and then fix in place with pins.

Stuff some modeling clay down into the butts of the ears and arrange them into position. To hold the skin of the ears up against the hidden plastic liners, use strips of stiff cardboard held in place with spring-loaded clothespins.

Drive pins wherever necessary to hold the skin in contact with depressions in the form. When the hide dries, it will hold in place especially if glue was applied earlier.

Step 5 — After the trophy has had a chance to dry and take a set, which usually requires a week or more, the finishing touches can be applied. The corners of the eyelids will usually have shrunk away from the eyes, and these openings can be filled with black shoe polish wax. The nose and tear ducts should be painted with artist's black oil paint. You probably should first take a close look at a picture of a deer before you apply the paint.

As a cross-check on the artistry and adequacy of the finishing touches of taxidermy, a fresh, new look at the results can be obtained by holding the mount in front of a mirror. This reverses the image and provides you with a new perspective. Whenever you create something, you become partially blind to the effect of that creation and how it will appear to other observers.

Index